Carp in North America

Frontispiece.—Carp in the fast lane with Jim Allen. (Courtesy, Illinois Department of Conservation.)

Carp in North America

Edwin L. Cooper, *Editor*

American Fisheries Society
Bethesda Maryland
1987

Publication of this book was made possible by support from the

Great Lakes Fisheries Development Foundation, Incorporated

and the

United States Fish and Wildlife Service

Address orders to
American Fisheries Society
5410 Grosvenor Lane, Suite 110
Bethesda, Maryland 20814, USA

Contents

Preface

Of all fishes, why a book on carp? And, why is one of North America's oldest and most respected professional societies producing a book on carp?

We have been asked those two questions often during the time that this book has been in preparation. Unfortunately, they reflect negative opinions of many anglers, and even many fishery biologists, toward a fish that should be thought of as an important fishery resource in North America.

Who hasn't heard some of the following ideas from anglers? "Carp are bad fish; they can survive even in sewers." "Carp are oily and taste terrible because they eat weeds and junk off the bottom." "Carp are lazy, sloth-like fish; no challenge to sportsmen." If you believe these myths, this book is intended to convince you that you are wrong on all counts. The carp is one of North America's most widely distributed and underutilized fishery resources. We believe that it deserves an enlightened consideration by anglers as an important fishery asset.

In the several chapters that follow, readers will learn about the carp's global distribution; how carp are perceived throughout Asia and Europe; when, why, and how carp were introduced to North America; the biology and behavior that enable carp to adapt to an extremely wide variety of habitats and conditions; how to angle for carp; existing and potential commercial fisheries for carp; the superb variety of ways to prepare and cook carp; how carp are being utilized today in North America; and how the negative image of carp can be modified.

We have no intention of convincing trout purists to trade their fly collections for a pound of white kernel corn and dough baits, nor of persuading bass enthusiasts to trade their bass boats for a lounge chair, a bite indicator, and a gas lantern. However, we do believe that objective readers will be convinced that carp deserve a better reputation.

I defy any confirmed fish connoisseur to read Vern Hacker's chapter on "Eating Carp" and not develop hunger pangs. Arnold Fritz's chapter on "Commercial Fishing for Carp" may stimulate entrepreneurial spirits to capitalize on the many potential markets for this species, markets that range from live fish to prepared products to supplies for fast-food restaurants.

Anglers, particularly those who have children in the family and live near waters containing carp, should become tempted to try the "prebaiting" techniques described by Ron Spitler in his chapter on "Sport Fishing for Carp." It is exciting to think that you could prebait an area and potentially have your youngsters battling a 10- to 20-pound carp from a safe location right on the shore.

Frank Panek's chapter on "Biology and Ecology of Carp" certainly defies any notions that carp are biologically inferior. These fish have evolved sophisticated adaptations for survival. Their ability to grow and reproduce in a broad array of habitats is cause for wonder and admiration, not disdain.

Tommy Sheddan reviews techniques for "Promoting Carp" in the final chapter. The ironic point that is driven home throughout the book is that the carp's image is tarnished by misconception, false accusation, and myth. Sheddan explains how these can be overcome.

The initiative and inspiration for this project came from William Lewis, President of the American Fisheries Society during 1982–1983. At the Society's 1982 annual meeting in South Carolina, Dr. Lewis established the Carp Committee and charged it to ". . . formulate an approach to the Society's contribution in stimulating greater utilization of the carp. . . ." I chaired the committee during 1982–1984, the developmental, formative period. Steve Flickinger was chairman during 1984–1986, the editorial, production period.

In addition to the five chapter authors mentioned above, Tom Gengerke served as managing editor and Edwin Cooper as editor-in-chief. Ed reviewed and edited the final manuscripts. Gary Edwards and Dave McDaniel generated and summarized a questionnaire to fishery agencies designed to elicit information on carp management ideas and needs. A media advisory panel, consisting of Homer Circle, Jerry Gibb, George Loechl, Norville Prosser, Mark Sosin, Doug Stange, and Ed Zern, was consulted for carp promotional ideas.

The American Fisheries Society's Executive Director Carl Sullivan and subsequent AFS presidents Janice Hughes, William Platts, and Johanna Reinhart continuously supported the Carp Committee's work. All of us who have had a hand in production of the book thank them for their enthusiastic support over the years.

Several individuals and agencies contributed photographs and drawings for this book. They are acknowledged with their respective illustrations, and we are grateful to all of them. Tim Paisley of The Carp Society was especially generous with his photos of the English carp-fishing scene.

Stop fishing around. Go carping!

BRUCE SHUPP
Albany, New York
January 15, 1987

Biology and Ecology of Carp

Frank M. Panek

Few freshwater fishes are as well known as the common carp (*Cyprinus carpio*). Also named the German carp, Israeli carp, or mirror carp, it is considered an excellent sport and table fish in Europe but an unwanted nuisance in sections of North America. The carp has been cultured throughout Eurasia for at least 4,000 years and much has been written on its diseases, nutrition, growth, genetics, and production.

Only a brief synopsis of the evolution, distribution, and life history of the carp is given here, with special mention of aspects that might be of interest to the general reader. More detailed information is contained in the many references found at the end of this chapter.

Evolution of Carp and its Relatives

The common carp is a minnow (family Cyprinidae), exotic to North America. Minnows are the largest family of freshwater fishes in the world with over 1,500 named species, among which are the many small shiners and chubs in North America and several large carps of Eurasia. Other close relatives are the suckers and redhorses of North America and the many characins of South America, often sold as tropical aquarium fishes.

The evolution and distribution of modern minnows are related to the movements of continents millions of years before the present. At the close of the Paleozoic Era 240 million years ago, the continents had drifted together to form the supercontinent Pangea, and the major groups of fishes were already well established. About 200 million years ago, Pangea began to split into northern and southern tiers. The northern tier, called Laurasia, contained the future North America, Europe, and northern Asia. To the south, Gondwanaland contained South America and Africa. North America lost its connections first with South America and then with Africa, and the north-south split was essentially complete 140 million years ago. About this time, both tiers began to break into eastern and western blocks along a line that would open to become the Atlantic Ocean. By 80 million years ago, both Americas were drifting "freely" to the west, and they reestablished tenuous connections with each other only in modern geological times. These continental movements led to the separation and further evolution of the many characins of South America and the many minnows of North America and Eurasia.

Evidence suggests that the common carp originated in the area of eastern Europe and western Asia after North America separated from Eurasia, and that the species spread throughout Europe and Asia from there. Many other carp-like fishes were evolving rapidly at the same time. Several of these larger carps, such

1

Two large exotic minnows that have become established in North America are the common carp (top, here drawn from a 1½-inch-long specimen) and the goldfish (middle). The shorthead redhorse (bottom) is a native member of the closely related sucker family. These paintings were done by Ellen Edmonson for New York State's watershed surveys of 1926–1939. (Courtesy, New York Department of Environmental Conservation.)

as the grass carp, the bighead carp, and the crucian carp (goldfish), are now intensively cultured throughout China for food and as ornamental fishes. The absence of native carp-like fishes from Australia (carp have been introduced there) is explained by the separation of that continent from Eurasia before the carp ancestors had evolved.

Original Range and Dispersal

The original range of the common carp probably was limited to the Asian watersheds of the Black, Caspian, and Aral seas. It may have been present in portions of western Europe, in the Volga River, and in eastern Asia from the Amur River southward to Burma. However, transfers of carp from the Danube River to Greece and Italy during the Roman Empire and the widespread culture of carp in monastic ponds throughout Europe during the Middle Ages have obscured its original geographic range. There is no evidence to support the common belief that it was introduced to Europe from an original range in China.

Carp were probably first introduced to England in 1496 and to Ireland during the reign of James I (1603–1625). Its cultural importance to England was indicated in records of King Henry VIII, for in 1532 various rewards were paid to persons bringing ''carpes to the King.'' In Holland, carp were often kept for months in cellars and fed milk and bread to be fattened for the table.

The first introduction of carp to North America did not occur until the 1800s, stimulated by interest in this fish by many immigrants from Europe. Details of this introduction are given in the chapter ''Commercial Fishing for Carp.''

Body Shape, Color, and Scale Pattern

The common carp has many features in common with other minnows: a Weberian apparatus, cycloid scales, pharyngeal teeth in the throat, but no teeth on the jaws. All minnows lack true spines, but the carp has the first ray of the dorsal and anal fins modified into a hard, serrated bony structure. These spines can inflict a deep, painful wound on the careless fish handler.

Whereas most minnows are usually less than 5 inches long, the common carp, like the squawfishes and some other minnows of western North America, often exceeds 2 feet in length and 10 pounds in weight. It is a robust fish whose body height is about one-fourth its length. The body is laterally compressed. A small triangular head tapers steeply to a blunt snout with a thick nose plate covered by very sensitive skin known as ''carp's tongue.'' The small and horizontal mouth, located below the snout, is protrusible and has no teeth. There are two barbels (fleshy projections) on each side of the upper jaw; the posterior barbels are usually longer than the anterior.

The goldfish is another exotic minnow with a robust body and an elongate dorsal fin similar to the carp's. However, it differs from the carp by lacking barbels around the mouth, and its pharyngeal teeth are not molar-like as in the carp. The pharyngeal teeth of the carp are well adapted for crushing and grinding food.

The color and scale pattern of the carp are highly variable, depending on the amount of genetic selection that has occurred. The color of the wild type is usually olive-green on the back shading to yellowish on the belly, and the fins are often reddish. Wild carp are fully scaled. Domesticated carp, selected for ornamental

A mirror carp caught by Peter Wright in England. Note the few very large scales along the midbody. (Courtesy, Tim Paisley.)

purposes, often show a wide range of white, gold, and black colors (the koi of Hawaii and China), and they may be completely scaled, have only a few isolated large scales (the mirror carp), or be almost scaleless (leather carp).

In large populations of carp, many unusual patterns of scalation and color occur infrequently along with the predominant wild type. In the British Isles, individual carp have been seen with glittering gold stripes on one side and pale blue on the other side. Mirror carp are sometimes seen in waters of North America.

Sensory Adaptations of Carp

Much of the ecological survival of the common carp has been attributed to its well-developed senses of hearing, smell, and taste. The aquatic environment apparently poses no obstacles to the development of senses of high acuity and discrimination.

The carp's sense of hearing is certainly improved over that of many other fishes by the evolutionary development of the Weberian apparatus. This structural adaptation is made up of a series of small bones and ligaments connecting the swim bladder with the inner ear. The usual function of the gas-filled swim bladder is to regulate buoyancy. In the carp, the swim bladder also acts as a resonating chamber for sound waves reaching it. These amplified vibrations are then carried to the brain, allowing the fish to respond to lower sound levels and wider ranges of sound waves than fishes not having such an apparatus.

The carp also has a well-developed sense of smell. Water enters an olfactory bulb through paired openings, the nares, carrying odorous materials to receptor cells that are embedded in the epithelium of the nasal cavity. Although it is not clear whether or not the acuity of the sense of smell is related to the number of receptor cells in the epithelium, it is well known that the carp has an acute and discriminating sense of smell.

Some minnows (and presumably the carp also) have used this acute sense of smell to activate a unique alarm system for the avoidance of predators. Large cells located in the skin release sensory chemicals (allomones) into the water when the skin is damaged by a predator. When these allomones are smelled by other minnows, the school scatters and seeks cover. This scattering response helps to increase survival of the rest of the school.

The sense of taste in carp is similar to that of higher animals. Specialized taste buds in the skin of the snout, mouth, lips, and throat are connected to the brain by special nerves. Tests have shown that carp can discriminate between salty, bitter, and sweet substances, as well as between many extracts of fish skin and other fish tissues. Anglers rely on this fine taste discrimination in the preparation of successful baits for carp.

Preferred Habitat

Carp occur in a wide range of habitats from clear mountain lakes to some of North America's most degraded rivers. They are found in the Great Lakes, large reservoirs, shallow ponds, swamps and bogs, large slow-moving rivers, fast-flowing streams, and even some tidal rivers and creeks.

Carp generally prefer shallow, weedy habitats with sufficient structure to afford protection and cover. For the most part, they seek quiet, shallow waters with muddy or sandy bottoms over which they can browse for food. They can be observed during daylight hours in protected bays and flats and around shoals

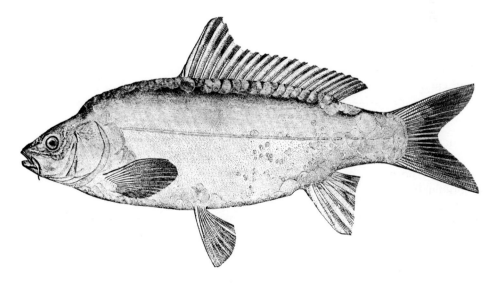

Leather carp, a nearly scaleless variety of the common carp. This drawing is from an 1890 Bulletin of the U.S. Fish Commission.

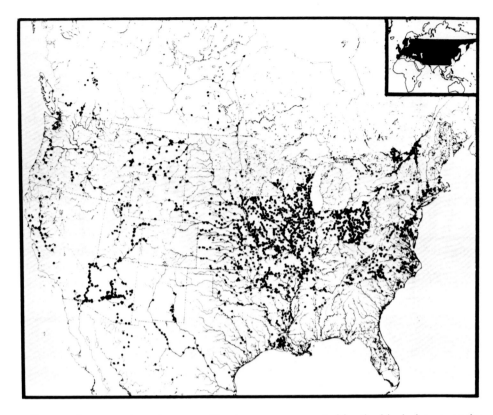

Few north temperate waters are without carp, as suggested by the black dots over the map of North America and the black swath across Europe and Asia. (From "Atlas of North American Freshwater Fishes," edited by D. S. Lee and others; courtesy, North Carolina State Museum of Natural History.)

adjacent to the security of deeper water. Although carp are rarely found at depths greater than 98 feet, deep-water areas may be sought in the winter when surface temperatures become uncomfortably cold.

The species is highly competitive and can quickly establish populations in new, unexploited, and disturbed habitats. The carp's ability to flourish in waters environmentally incapable of supporting gamefish populations is demonstrated by its broad and stable distribution in North America.

Environmental Factors

The widespread distribution of carp in North America is partially due to its broad temperature tolerance. It can be caught during winter in ice-covered lakes and can survive short periods of time at a temperature of 106°F. However, the optimal temperature for carp is 66°F, similar to the optimum for many fishes in north temperate waters. Carp in northern waters begin active feeding when spring water temperatures reach 39°F. At temperatures above 72°F, any restriction of food supply influences growth rate, and carp can survive extended periods at temperatures above 90°F, only if the food supply is nearly unlimited. The upper lethal limit has been variously reported between 97 and 106°F.

Temperature also affects the amount of dissolved oxygen necessary for survival of carp, the oxygen requirement of the fish increasing with a rise in temperature. Compared to many temperate game fishes, carp have a low oxygen consumption rate. They are moderately tolerant of low dissolved oxygen conditions, although oxygen concentrations less than 3 parts per million (ppm) cause decreases in feeding and growth.

Part of the carp's tolerance of poorly oxygenated water is due to its ability to load its blood hemoglobin at low levels of oxygen and concurrent high levels of carbon dioxide. In this respect, carp are superior to fishes such as trout, but are not as tolerant as bullheads. Carp commonly survive in warm water at a dissolved oxygen concentration of 2 ppm or less, a condition that would be fatal to trout. Carp experience respiratory difficulty at dissolved oxygen concentrations below 4.5 ppm.

Carp are extremely tolerant of turbidity caused by suspended clay, silt, or other particulate matter. The lethal level of turbidity for carp approaches 165,000 ppm, several times the amount that restricts light penetration and limits productivity of lakes. Because carp can feed more efficiently in the dark by smell and taste than many sight-feeders, they enjoy a competitive advantage in turbid waters. Such conditions commonly occur in new reservoirs with excessive erosion of clay soils.

Low tolerance of salinity is one factor that limits the distribution of carp along

Carp have a reputation for inhabiting polluted streams, but the species can be caught in many idyllic settings as well. (Courtesy, Tim Paisley.)

seacoasts. Although carp can survive a rapid change to a salinity of about 1,000 ppm ($^1/_{30}$ normal sea water), a solution of 1,500 to 2,000 ppm is lethal in $1^1/_2$ days. High salinities cause excretory problems and probably interfere with water balance. Hence, carp are rarely found in brackish waters, and do not freely disperse across marine barriers as trout and salmon do.

Sexual Maturity and Reproduction

Carp mature and spawn at different ages, according to sex and growth rate. Fast-growing males may mature in 1 year, but females in populations of slowly growing fish may take up to 5 years before maturing. The average male is 2 years old and 12 inches long at maturity; females are usually 3 years old and 17 inches long at their first spawning.

Records from North America and Europe indicate that spawning is essentially restricted to fresh water, although limited spawning has been reported from brackish water. In rivers, as the water warms to about 41°F in spring and early summer, carp often migrate long distances to find suitable spawning conditions, and can be seen racing upstream across shallow gravel bars. In large reservoirs, carp congregate in overwintering areas adjacent to shallows where they will spawn, often using the same spawning areas year after year. Most spawning occurs in late spring or early summer when the water temperature reaches 63°F. Variations in climate over the extended range of this fish in North America thus result in carp spawning from March in the south through mid-August in the north.

Spawning behavior is not secretive, but occurs with much splashing about in water 1 to 2 feet deep. Spawning occurs both day and night over several weeks as the water warms from 63°F to 75°F, but will cease at temperatures above 81°F. Carp do not build nests nor do they protect their eggs or young. During spawning, one or more males pursue a female as eggs and milt are released into the water. The eggs sink and adhere to rooted vegetation, algae, or firm substrates. Eggs generally occur in clusters of several hundred; in areas of extensive spawning it is not uncommon to find 2,500 eggs per square yard of bottom.

In early spring, spawning habitats tend to be restricted to shallow bottomlands and marshes that warm rapidly, such as cattail marshes. In the Kuybyshev Reservoir of the Soviet Union, carp spawn over shallow flooded vegetation where temperatures are 59° in the morning but tend to rise above 63°F during midday. They also spawn later in deeper water at a temperature of about 52°F. These spawning conditions appear to be marginal for survival since experiments have shown that temperatures less than 61°F or greater than 79°F are lethal to carp eggs.

The lack of parental care is compensated for by the production of large numbers of eggs. Egg production is correlated with fish size such that larger fish generally produce more eggs. For instance, a 5-pound carp may produce half a million eggs and a 20-pound carp may spawn more than 2 million. The eggs are small, less than 0.1 inch in diameter. Eggs spawned by 2-year-old fish are often twice the size of those produced by 1-year-olds.

Eggs may develop to the "eyed" stage, when pigmented eyes are visible through the egg capsule, in 24 hours at a temperature of 70°F, and they can hatch in 6 days at a temperature of 63°F. The larvae at hatching are $^1/_4$ inch long. They are heavily pigmented on the head and back and prominently so along the belly.

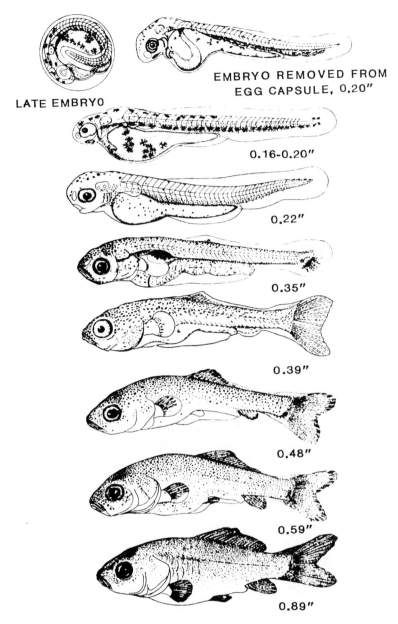

LATE EMBRYO

EMBRYO REMOVED FROM
EGG CAPSULE, 0.20"

0.16-0.20"

0.22"

0.35"

0.39"

0.48"

0.59"

0.89"

   Early developmental stages of carp from late embryo to a length of nearly 1 inch. (Modified from "Manual for Identification of Early Developmental Stages of Fishes of the Potomac River Estuary," by A. J. Lippson and R. L. Moran; courtesy, Versar, ESM Operations.)

During the first few days of life, these small larvae remain attached to vegetation until they have completely absorbed their yolk sacs. This generally occurs by the fifth day. Most carp can be readily distinguished from other fishes when they reach $3/8$ inch in length, and they develop barbels at $1/2$ inch. The fins are fully formed and some scales are evident at 1 inch.

In general, small carp remain in areas protected from wave action and predation. Eggs hatched in cattail and similar marshes are often at an advantage over those spawned in open lake waters. Not only do cattails and bulrushes break up wave action, but the shallow protected waters of the marsh are often significantly warmer than lake water. Young fish, remaining in these areas for most of the summer, can grow rapidly to 4 inches by October.

Young carp are seldom observed; the fish prefer to hide rather than find safety in flight. They will often bury themselves in mud or sand as a means of avoiding predaceous birds. Such behavior, in addition to high fecundity, enable carp to rapidly establish populations in suitable habitats.

Age and Growth

While stories of 100-year-old carp from Fontainebleau and Chantilly of France are surely fables, carp have been known to survive up to 47 years in captivity. Information on the longevity of wild carp is questionable in view of the inaccuracy of estimating age by means of annual growth marks on scales or bones. These "year marks" were noted on scales of carp as early as 1898, but more critical studies in recent years have shown that they are quite unreliable after fish reach an age of 10 or 15 years, and investigators generally underestimate the true age of older fish. Although many biologists now believe that wild carp seldom live longer than 20 years, the English have photographic records of carp that have been caught and recaught over periods approaching 50 years.

Carp sometimes become very large. A world record carp of about 82 pounds was reported from Pretoria, South Africa, and a North American carp of 74 pounds was taken in 1963 from Pelahatchie Lake, Mississippi.

Growth rates of carp depend upon a variety of biological and environmental factors. In addition to genetically defined limits, growth can be influenced by temperature, length of the growing season, water chemistry, and the availability of food. Wild carp grow more slowly than many of the unique strains developed through selective breeding. Mirror and leather carp provide more flesh per fish length than wild parental stocks.

Growth of wild fish is affected by biotic factors. High population density is usually accompanied by a slower growth rate. It has been suggested in recent studies that high densities lead to excessive excretion of certain metabolites that have a negative effect on carp growth.

Considerable variation in growth rate of carp occurs across North America. This variation may reflect geography or environmental and biotic conditions existing at each of the locations. Generally, male and female carp exhibit similar growth. For the most part, both sexes grow very rapidly during their first few years of life. Growth tends to slow when they reach maturity and more energy is diverted into reproduction.

Food and Feeding

Carp feed at different levels in the water from the bottom to the surface. Most often, they root around in silty bottoms in water less than 10 feet deep, but they also utilize plankton suspended in midwater and sometimes eat insects or plankton caught in the surface film. When feeding on the bottom, they will suck up quantities of silt, then spit it out and select insects or other items of food from the water. Large carp can effectively penetrate 5 inches into silty bottoms in search of food. Such feeding behavior often leaves submerged aquatic plants uprooted or the bottom pockmarked. Some sorting of food is done in the mouth and throat, but a large quantity of detritus is often found in the intestine, indicating that this sorting is not very effective.

Most active feeding occurs at sunrise and sunset when waters are calm and there is less disturbance by potential predators. A noisy boat fisherman may scatter the carp from its feeding grounds to seek cover in heavy vegetation or deep water.

Young carp feed primarily on animal foods such as small crustacea, snails, and midge larvae. Zooplankton selected from the water column are, at times, an important source of nutrition. At Cayuga Lake, New York, young carp were observed to graze along the rootlets of duckweed or along the stems and leaves of various aquatic plants. However, actual plant material represented a small portion of the diet.

Adult carp are truly omnivorous, consuming varying amounts of plant and animal foods. Plant material in the diet varies among populations and includes both rooted plants and algae. Organic debris can also be an important part of the carp's diet, ranging from 24% in a Colorado river to 61% in Lewis and Clark Lake, South Dakota. It is believed that aquatic vegetation is not actively sought by carp for food, but it can be consumed in large quantities while the fish search for aquatic insects. Dominant animal foods of adult carp include midge larvae, crustaceans, small snails, and freshwater clams. Fish and fish eggs have seldom been noted in carp stomachs. Carp in lakes and ponds differ from those in streams by showing preference for the abundant planktonic crustaceans typical of lake communities.

The turbidity caused by feeding carp and the uprooting of vegetation have been causes of complaints against this fish. It is not uncommon to see disturbances of plant communities in waters with substantial carp populations. Uprooting behavior was observed in Cayuga Lake, New York. There, a large mass of plant debris consisting of pondweeds and other aquatic plants accumulated in a windrow near an area where a large school of carp had fed for several days. Plants were completed uprooted from many areas of the bottom. However, most of these areas were eventually revegetated, leading observers to conclude in 1928 that "the gustatory greediness of carp populations are not decidedly injurious to the plants." More recent studies have shown carp to be detrimental to plant communities, and disturbances of spawning and nursery areas of game fishes have been documented.

Parasites and Diseases

Carp have a variety of parasites and diseases that can cause different responses ranging from rapid death to chronic illness. As an exotic species, carp are partly responsible for the introduction of several parasites to North American waters from Europe and Asia. Of the 170 kinds of parasites known from carp in North America, 138 were introduced. These parasitic organisms include algae, fungi, protozoans, flatworms, tapeworms, leeches, and crustaceans.

The most common parasites of carp include some protozoans, flatworms, and crustaceans. Two common protozoans often cause a condition known as "blue-slime disease." Another common protozoan, known as "ich" to tropical fish hobbyists, causes destruction of skin, often leading to secondary infections by an aquatic fungus which is often fatal. Trypanoplasmosis, a form of sleeping sickness, is caused by another protozoan having a whip-like flagellum. This blood parasite uses the fish leech as an intermediate host and means of infestation.

Carp can be infested with a variety of flatworms and roundworms. These cause considerable damage in cultured carp by eroding gill filaments. Similar conditions are known to occur in high-density wild populations. The larvae of some flatworms can be found in most tissues, where they accumulate to such an extent that they interfere with the carp's metabolism. Their movements through tissues also cause mechanical damage and hemorrhage. Some flatworms parasitize the eye lens and cause blindness. Roundworms usually reside in the intestinal tract, but may be found in almost every organ.

Crustacean parasites are common in both cultured and wild carp. Commonly referred to as an anchor worm, one of these copepods burrows under the skin and causes considerable damage to the underlying tissues. Red blood cells accumulate at the site of the wound and the skin eventually takes on an appearance typical of hemorrhagic septicemia. This may lead to infectious dropsy, ulcer disease, and red-mouth disease.

In addition to diseases caused by parasites and pathogens, diet can affect carp health. The knothead malformation of carp, described from the Illinois River and at Cayuga and Owasco lakes in New York, results from a vitamin D deficiency. Fish showing this condition do not grow as rapidly as healthy carp.

While there is much information available on the diseases and parasites of cultured carp, there is little information about wild populations. In fact, most infectious diseases described for cultured carp do not show up in wild populations except at unusually high population densities. Only under crowded conditions do these diseases have a profound effect on health and survival. It does not appear that disease and parasites play an important role in controlling wild populations.

Effects of Carp on Other Fishes

Carp are found in just about every freshwater habitat. Because they eat a wide variety of plants and animals, they often make up a large proportion of the total weight of fish present. In many North American lakes and reservoirs, carp populations average about 100 pounds per acre, and reach densities of 420 pounds per acre in some northern waters. Predatory game fishes such as largemouth bass, walleye, and northern pike seldom exceed 15 pounds per acre. Where conditions are suitable for carp, they often displace other fishes through competition for food and space.

Carp populations affect other fishes mainly through their impacts on aquatic plants and water turbidity through their feeding behavior. The uprooting and consumption of aquatic plants by carp may interfere with the spawning of fishes such as northern pike or yellow perch that use plant beds as sites for egg laying. Carp may also cause nesting fishes to desert their nests, exposing eggs and fry to predation. A lack of vegetation decreases cover and increases predation on the young of fishes such as catfishes and sunfishes.

Increased turbidity caused by the feeding behavior of carp decreases the feeding efficiency of sunfishes and largemouth bass that feed largely by sight. Increased turbidity may decrease the productivity of rooted aquatic plants by reducing light penetration, but carp may also cause the bloom of noxious algae by recycling nutrients from bottom muds through their feeding behavior.

Carp Population Control

The control of carp has included seining, destruction of spawning habitat by drawdown, construction of fish barrier dams, introduction of predators, and uses of fish toxicants, electricity, nets, and baited traps. Each of these techniques has had varying degrees of success. Since many of them are nonselective, their effects on other fishes often limit their use.

The most widely used techniques have included combinations of netting, fish toxicants, and fish barriers. Commercial fishing is often encouraged in waters with high-density carp populations. These fisheries may reduce carp densities temporarily, but carp populations often rebound once the commercial fishery falls to unprofitable levels.

The use of fish toxicants such as rotenone and antimycin in carp spawning areas has been effective in partially reducing carp populations in some waters. However, the loss of other species and the consequent poor public relations resulting from such treatment often argues against this practice.

Fish barrier screens can be used effectively to keep carp from spawning marshes or to keep them out of reclaimed waters. Barriers are most commonly used at wildlife refuges to keep carp out of waterfowl production areas where they can do considerable damage. Treatment with rotenone killed 95% of the carp in a Utah bird refuge. In combination with screening, this provided effective carp control for 2 years.

Another widely used technique for carp control is water level regulation. Its success depends upon exposing spawning areas and eggs to air, stranding small fish in vegetation and shallow pools, and concentrating fish in open waters where they are vulnerable to exploitation. A combination of drawdown and commercial fishing was effective in controlling carp in Elephant Butte Reservoir, New Mexico.

References

Balon, E. K. 1974. Domestication of the carp, *Cyprinus carpio* L. Royal Ontario Museum, Life Sciences Miscellaneous Publication, Toronto, Canada. 37 p.

Berry, C. R., Jr. 1982. Behavior and ecology of carp in the Bear River Migratory Bird Refuge. Utah State University, Utah Cooperative Fishery Research Unit, Final Completion Report. Logan, Utah. 55 p.

Black, E. C. 1953. Upper lethal temperatures of some British Columbia freshwater fishes. Journal of the Fisheries Research Board of Canada 10:196.

Black, V. S. 1951. Osmotic regulation in teleost fishes. Publications of the Ontario Fisheries Research Laboratory 71:53–89.

Borzenko, M. P. 1926. Materials for biology of the carp (*Cyprinus carpio* Linnaeus). Bulletin of the Ichthyological Laboratory, Baku 2(1):5–132.

Bowen, J. T. 1970. A history of fish culture as related to the development of fishery programs. Pages 71–93 *in* N. G. Benson, editor. A century of fisheries in North America. American Fisheries Society, Special Publication 7, Bethesda, Maryland. 330 p.

Breder, C. M., Jr., and D. E. Rosen. 1966. Modes of reproduction in fishes. Natural History Press, Garden City, New Jersey. 941 p.

Cahoon, R. M. 1953. Commercial carp removal on Lake Mattamuskeet, North Carolina. Journal of Wildlife Management 17:312–317.

Carlander, K. D. 1955. The standing crop of fish in lakes. Journal of the Fisheries Research Board of Canada 12:543–570.

Chiba, K. 1966. A study on the influence of oxygen concentration on the growth of juvenile common carp. Bulletin of the Freshwater Fisheries Research Laboratory (Tokyo) 1501:35–47.

Courtenay, W. R., Jr., D. A. Hensley, J. N. Taylor and J. A. McCann. 1984. Distribution of exotic fishes in the continental United States. Pages 41–71 *in* W. R. Courtenay, Jr. and J. R. Stauffer, editors. Distribution, biology and management of exotic fishes. Johns Hopkins University Press, Baltimore, Maryland. 430 p.

Crivelli, A. 1981. The biology of the common carp (*Cyprinus carpio*) in Camarque, southern France. Journal of Fish Biology 18:271–290.

Darlington, P. J., Jr. 1957. Zoogeography: the geographical distribution of animals. John Wiley & Sons, New York, New York. 675 p.

Eder, S., and C. A. Carlson. 1977. Food habits of carp and white suckers in the South Platte and St. Urain rivers and Goosequill Pond, Weld County, Colorado. Transactions of the American Fisheries Society 106:339–346.

English, T. S. 1952. Growth studies of the carp, *Cyprinus carpio* Linnaeus, in Clear Lake, Iowa. Iowa State Journal of Science 24:537–540.

Haines, T. A. 1973. Effects of nutrient enrichment and a roughfish population (carp) on a gamefish population (smallmouth bass). Transactions of the American Fisheries Society 101:350–352.

Hoffman, G. L. 1967. Parasites of North American freshwater fishes. University of California Press, Berkeley, California. 486 p.

Johnson, P. B., and A. D. Hasler. 1977. Winter aggregations of carp as revealed by ultrasonic tracking. Transactions of the American Fisheries Society 106:556–565.

King, D., and G. Hunt. 1967. Effects of carp on vegetation in a Lake Erie marsh. Journal of Wildlife Management 31:181–188.

Kirpichnikov, U. S. 1966. Selective breeding of carp and intensification of fish breeding in ponds. Bulletin of the State Scientific Research Institute for Lake and River Fisheries 61:1–249. (Translated from Russian: Israel program for Scientific Translation, Jerusalem.)

Lippson, A. J., and R. L. Moran. 1974. Manual for identification of early developmental stages of fishes on the Potomac River estuary. Martin Marietta Corporation prepared for Maryland Power Plant Siting Program, PPSP-MP-13, Annapolis, Maryland. 282 p.

Loeb, H. A. 1960. Reactions of aquarium carp to food and flavors. New York Fish and Game Journal 7:60–71.

McCrimmon, H. R. 1968. Carp in Canada. Bulletin of the Fisheries Research Board of Canada 165. 93 p.

Osipov, V. B. 1979. A contribution to the ecology of the carp, *Cyprinus carpio,* in the Cheremshan Arm at Kuybyshev Reservoir. Journal of Ichthyology 19(5):151–154. (English translation of Voprosy Ikhtiologii.)

Plehn, M. 1924. Praktikum der Fischkrankheiten. Handbuch der Binnenfischerei Mitteleuropas, volume 1:301–470.

Purkett, C. A., Jr. 1957. Growth of the fishes in the Salt River, Missouri. Transactions of the American Fisheries Society 87:116–131.

Schaeperclaus, W. 1933. Textbook of pond culture. U.S. Fish and Wildlife Service, Fishery Leaflet 311. 260 p.

Sigler, W. F. 1958. The ecology and use of carp in Utah. Utah Agricultural Experiment Station Bulletin 405. 63 p.

Smallwood, W. M., and M. L. Smallwood. 1929. The German carp, an invited immigrant. Scientific Monthly 29:394–401.

Swee, U. B., and H. R. McCrimmon. 1966. Reproductive biology of the carp, *Cyprinus carpio* L., in Lake St. Lawrence, Ontario. Transactions of the American Fisheries Society 95:372–380.

Threinen, E. W., and W. T. Helm. 1954. Experiments and observations designed to show carp destruction of aquatic vegetation. Journal of Wildlife Management 18:247–250.

Wallen, I. E. 1951. The direct effect of turbidity on fishes. Oklahoma Agricultural and Mechanical University Biological Bulletin 48(2):1–27.
Wohlfarth, G., M. Lahman and R. Moav. 1963. Genetic improvement of carp. IV. Leather and line carp in fish ponds in Israel. Bamidgeh 15(1):3–8. (Ministry of Agriculture, Fisheries Division, Israel.)
Yarrell, W. 1936. A history of British fishes. John Van Voorst, London, England. 408 p.

Commercial Fishing for Carp

Arnold W. Fritz

Prior to 1900, most native North American fishes were viewed primarily as valuable and vital food resources. Most of the fishes that are designated as sport or game fishes today were all harvested commercially, including the various basses, sunfishes, crappies, pikes, walleye, yellow perch, and lake trout. These fishes, in addition to others such as buffalofishes, suckers, catfishes, bullheads, sturgeons, freshwater drum, and paddlefish, were harvested by the millions of pounds. They were shipped by railroad cars to markets in large cities where they were an important and inexpensive food resource.

Due to this tremendous harvest, many people within the United States began to express grave concerns about the declining stocks of river and lake fishes. A large supply was considered most essential to meet the food needs of the nation's rapidly expanding population. In response to these concerns, Congress authorized President Ulysses S. Grant in 1871 to appoint the United States Fish Commission to oversee the nation's fisheries interests. Following its formation, one of the first tasks undertaken by the Commission was to consider the question of what species to introduce to bolster the nation's supply of food fishes. In the 1874 report of the Commission, S.F. Baird expressed the following opinions about carp under the title "Fishes Especially Worthy of Cultivation."

> Sufficient attention has not been paid in the United States to the introduction of the European carp as a food fish, and yet it is quite safe to say that there is no other species that promises so great a return in limited waters. It has the preeminent advantage over such fish as the black bass, trout, grayling, and others in that it is a vegetable feeder, and although not disdaining animal matters, can thrive very well upon aquatic vegetation alone. On this account, it can be kept in tanks, and small ponds, and a very much larger weight obtained than the case of other kinds indicated. It is on this account that its culture has been continued for centuries.

Two years later (1876), Professor Baird enumerated other good qualities of carp such as high fecundity, adaptability to the processes of artificial propagation, hardiness in all stages of growth, adaptability to environmental conditions unfavorable to equally palatable American fishes, rapid growth, harmlessness in its relation to other fishes, ability to populate waters to their greatest extent, and good table qualities. By 1877, it was evident that the Commission was convinced that the carp was the species most suited for pond culture when Professor Baird stated, "as some varieties of carp have been developed and had their instinct of domestication established, while experiments on our indigenous species are scarcely yet tried, there is no reason why time should be lost with less proved fishes." The decision to import carp was undoubtedly reinforced by requests for their importation as early as 1876 from persons of European origin who were familiar with the carp as a good food fish. Requests for carp stocking continued to increase yearly and, in 1880, the Commission received 2,000 requests.

Convinced of the value of carp, the Commission imported in 1877, under the direction of Rudolph Hessel, 345 carp of different varieties (scaled, mirror, and leather). On May 26, 1877, these fish were placed in the Druid Hill Park ponds in Baltimore, Maryland, to be propagated by T.B. Ferguson, Maryland's fish commissioner. Since these ponds were insufficient to properly care for the carp, some of them were transferred the following year to the Babcock Lakes on the monument lot in Washington, D.C., to be cultured by Mr. Hessel.

Propagation and Stocking

There is some question as to who first imported and propagated carp in the United States. Several references credited Captain Henry Robinson of Newburgh, New York, with the first introduction in 1831 and 1832. Supposedly, some of the fish escaped from his pond, creating a carp fishery in the Hudson River. However, when Professor Baird of the U.S. Fish Commission examined some of these fish, then being sold on the New York markets, he indicated that they were not the common carp but rather goldfish. Quite likely the first successful importation of carp can be credited to Julius A. Poppe of Sonoma, California, He managed to transport only five small carp of an original purchase of 83 from Reinfeld, Germany, to his pond in 1872. These fish reproduced the following year and, shortly thereafter, Mr. Poppe developed a good business of selling carp to area farmers in southern California. He is also credited with the first shipment of carp to Honolulu and Central America.

Accounts of the first few years of propagating and stocking carp are found in various U.S. and state fish commission reports. In 1879, Rudolph Hessel produced 6,203 carp fingerlings in the Babcock ponds. These were shipped to 273 applicants in 24 states. About 6,000 fingerling carp were also produced in the Druid Hill ponds the same year. These were later stocked primarily in Maryland. One year later, 31,332 carp were shipped by the U.S. Fish Commission to 1,374 applicants. In 1882, carp production increased to 143,696 fish, distributed in small lots to 7,000 applicants. In 1883, about 260,000 carp were sent to 9,872 applicants in 298 of the 301 congressional districts and into 1,478 counties. During the years 1879 to 1896, the Fish Commission distributed approximately 2.4 million carp, some of which were sent to countries such as Canada, Costa Rica, Ecuador, and Mexico. But by 1897, the Commission discontinued the production and distribution of carp, because stocking requests for this fish were no longer being received.

Of those carp received by state fish commissions during the 1879–1885 period, some were redistributed, while others were retained to be propagated by the respective states. Within several years, these states were also involved in stocking millions of carp. In 1881, the Ohio State Fish Commission stocked carp into the Maumee River and Ten Mile Creek, tributaries of Lake Erie. Every major river in Illinois was stocked with carp in 1885, although carp had reportedly been taken from these waters in previous years. Fish rescue operations conducted by various states and the U.S. Fish Commission during the 1890–1920 period, particularly within the midwestern region of the United States, also resulted in hundreds of other waters being stocked with carp and other river fishes.

Within a few years after carp were first stocked, it appeared that the U.S. Fish Commission had indeed accomplished what it had set out to do. Many glowing accounts were received from the recipients of carp as to their rapid growth, reproductive potential, eating and sporting qualities, and worth to the common man. Newspapers and magazines were also loud in their praises of the carp.

Typical of the enthusiastic reception of carp was an article published in the Texas Farm and Ranch magazine: "Of the importance of this fish [carp] in the future food supply of Texas, too much cannot be said; and yet it would seem sufficient merely to state that in a pond only a few square rods in area the farmer can raise, without expense, more than sufficient carp to supply his family the year round. Indeed, we trust the day is not far off when the carp pond, shaded with big trees and willows, and decorated with rose bushes and flowers, will be the possession of every farmer who aspired to thrift, taste, and good living."

Commercial Harvest of Carp

It was inevitable that the carp would become significant components of fish populations in North America because of their high reproduction potential and adaptability to a wide variety of aquatic environments and water quality conditions. Within 4 years after the U.S. Fish Commission began stocking them, carp were being caught by commercial fishermen from the Illinois, Missouri, and Mississippi rivers and Lake Erie. By 1885, the health officer of the District of Columbia was inspecting carp from the Potomac River that were being sold in the city's fish markets. The same year, a commercial fisherman took the first carp from Lake Ontario.

Each year, federal and state fish commissions continued to document the rapid population expansion of carp throughout the country. By 1891 carp were becoming quite abundant in Illinois streams, resulting in some large catches being made by commercial fishermen. Dr. S. P. Bartlett reported that one fisherman from Merodosia, Illinois, caught 27,000 pounds of carp in two 900-yard seine hauls in 1893. He received 7 to 10 cents per pound for each carp weighing 7 pounds or more, and 3 to 5 cents per pound for those under that size.

In 1893, H. M. Smith investigated the fyke net catches of the Atlantic and Pacific coast regions. He noted that commercial fishermen caught and marketed 5,800 pounds and 42,115 pounds of carp from these two regions, respectively. Those taken from the Pacific region undoubtedly came from the successful introduction of carp into California in 1872. Because carp were becoming commonplace in fish markets of the United States, Smith noted that "carp has had sufficient abundance in public waters to warrant prosecution of a special fishery or give the fish a conspicuous position in the fish markets of the country. Large quantities are being taken from Lake Erie and other lakes and rivers of the interior states, and carp are now regularly exposed for sale and usually cited in market quotations in all the large cities." He later reported that 46,798 pounds of carp, valued at $1,715 were being taken from the waters of New Jersey, Pennsylvania, Maryland, and Virginia.

In 1894, 627,000 pounds of carp valued at $16,245 were taken from Lake Erie by fishermen from Michigan, Ohio, New York, and Pennsylvania. It is likely that these fish resulted from plantings made by the Ohio State Fish Commission in 1881. The 1900 Lake Erie carp catch was later estimated to be 4.6 million pounds. Whether this poundage was taken strictly by United States fishermen or included the Canadian catch of carp is not known for certain.

The populations of carp virtually exploded during the 1890s in the Illinois and Mississippi rivers. In 1895, four fishing firms in Havana, Illinois, indicated they harvested 151,500 pounds of carp in 6 months from the Illinois River. These fish were shipped to markets in New York, Boston, and St. Louis. From this date, the annual carp harvest in Illinois continued to exceed that of the native buffalofishes. In 1895 and 1896, the U.S. Fish Commission gathered information pertaining to the commercial harvest of carp from 20 of the states, chiefly within the Mississippi River basin. They determined that 1.45 million pounds of carp were harvested from this region; the value of the harvest was $37,683 or 2.6 cents per pound. They also noted that Illinois had the largest inland commercial fisheries, producing 9.76 million pounds of fish, of which 860,300 pounds were carp. For the year ending February 1897, about 3.7 million pounds of carp were harvested from the Illinois River alone. Two years later, the Illinois River harvest of carp had increased to 6.3 million pounds and was valued at $189,981. This 1-year catch of carp in 1899 was greater than the total annual harvest of all commercial species now being taken in all of Illinois.

When the first major survey of the commercial fisheries in the United States was taken in 1880, the carp was not mentioned. However, in 1908, a similar survey indicated that 42.76 million pounds of carp valued at $1.14 million were taken by commercial fishermen in the United States. Of this, 39.82 million pounds were taken from the north-central states of Iowa, Illinois, Ohio, Michigan, Wisconsin, Missouri, and Minnesota. Fifty-one percent, or 21.64 million pounds of carp valued at $574,000, were taken by Illinois commercial fishermen, followed by Ohio with a harvest of 11%, or 7.16 million pounds worth $129,000. Not only did this survey indicate the greatest harvest of carp ever achieved, it documented the tremendous population explosion occurring within the short span of 29 years from the first stocking of this fish.

Harvest data for carp in the early 1900s are not well reported but, by 1930, the annual United States production of carp had declined sharply to about 23 million pounds. The following year, production declined to about 17 million pounds, establishing an all-time production low for carp. This decline was probably due more to the disfavor of the carp as a food fish than a real decrease in the carp population.

Although the commercial catch in the Mississippi River basin was not resurveyed again until around 1950, the overall United States harvest data available for the 1940s indicated that the catch of carp had increased slightly from the 1931 low. With minor fluctuations, the annual carp catch continued to increase gradually until 1955, when it again peaked at 36 million pounds, having a wholesale value of $1,628,000. From that time up to 1977, the last year that national catch data are available, the harvest of carp gradually declined to slightly less than 25 million pounds.

Within the continental United States and Canada, the Mississippi River basin ranks first (60 to 75%) in the pounds of carp harvested each year. Second in rank

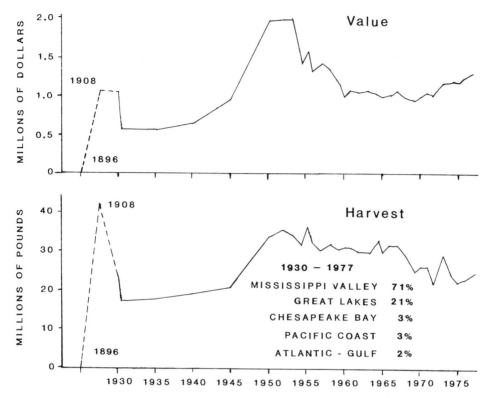

The largest commercial harvests of carp in the United States occurred in the early 1900s. During the decade after World War II, annual catches reached 36 million pounds worth $2 million, but have been lower since. Over 70% of the recorded U.S. catch has been taken in the Mississippi River basin since 1930. Additional Canadian harvests of carp from the Great Lakes have been about equal to those from the Chesapeake Bay area. (Data have been compiled from federal, state, and provincial reports.)

is the Great Lakes region, followed by the Chesapeake Bay and Pacific coast regions.

In Canada, the history of commercial carp fishing, particularly in the Great Lakes region, has closely paralleled that of the United States since 1900. Peak carp production occurred in 1914, when 2.5 million pounds were taken, principally from Canadian waters of Lake Erie and Lake St. Clair. Since 1914, one million pounds or more have been taken from these waters during the years 1915 to 1918, 1933 to 1935, and 1953 to 1959. Since 1959, the commercial harvest of carp from the region has also decreased rather steadily to a low of about 79,000 pounds in 1980. Until 1970, when Lake St. Clair's commercial fishery was closed due to mercury contamination of its fishes, this lake, along with Lakes Erie, Ontario, and Huron, produced the bulk of the carp harvested commercially in Canada. Substantial harvest of carp is also taken from the more southerly latitudes of British Columbia, Saskatchewan, Manitoba, and Quebec.

Although detailed data on carp harvested in Canada are not usually available, the following information was obtained through generous responses to a mail survey conducted by the author in 1983. The province of Saskatchewan reported

Large seine nets are set around expected concentrations of carp and then pulled to shore at each end. (Courtesy, Illinois Natural History Survey.)

an annual carp harvest decreasing from 848,679 pounds in 1974 to 186,300 pounds in 1983, these fish coming from Pasque Lake, Lost Mountain Lake, and Katepwa Lake. Lakes Manitoba, Winnipeg, and Winnipegosis in the province of Manitoba produced a carp harvest ranging from 53,673 pounds in 1976 to 1.86 million pounds in 1981. The British Columbia carp fishery is confined to the lower Fraser River. The St. Lawrence River, Outaonais River, and Lakes St. Pierre, St. Louis, and St. Francois support the primary commercial carp fisheries in Quebec.

Methods of Harvesting

Seining is the most frequently used method in North America to harvest carp in the northern states and Canadian provinces; however, in the southern and midwestern states, trammel nets, gill nets, and hoop nets are preferred. In some waters, type of gear and mesh size are restricted by regulations aimed at minimizing incidental capture of game fishes. In other instances, choice of gear is based on the intended capture of other, more valuable, commercial species, in the course of which carp are also taken. Even though the price paid for carp is low relative to that for other species, carp are usually kept and sold to help pay for operating costs.

Commercial fishermen have the greatest respect for the wariness of carp, and often fish for them only during certain periods of the year when their behavior makes them more vulnerable to capture. During the spring, when carp move into shallow waters to feed and spawn, large tonnages can often be taken by seine or wing nets with lead-netting. Carp are also susceptible to capture in cold water, either prior to freeze-up or under ice in lakes and reservoirs, where they often form large schools that can be detected by various sonar equipment. Before freeze-up, large catches are often taken by seines pulled by long white ropes, which aid in herding schools of carp. When there is ice cover, a series of holes is drilled in the ice. A long rope, attached to a board, is threaded from hole to hole. Once the rope is stretched out, it is attached to the seine, which is pulled under the ice to encircle the fish. On occasion, such seine hauls may yield several hundred thousand pounds. When large poundages of carp are bagged up, their swimming action frequently circulates enough water to melt the ice and to erode a deep hole in the lake bottom.

A large portion of the commercial carp harvest of the southern and midwestern states is taken by trammel nets, gill nets, and hoop nets set in areas of known carp concentrations or movement. On other occasions, trammel nets, gill nets, or variations of these nets are set around various types of cover preferred by carp, and the fish are then scared into the nets by creating loud noises with toilet bowl plungers or by beating on the water and the sides of the boat.

Chumming, illegal in some states, is another method of increasing the harvest of carp. Grains such as corn or barley, soaked several days to sour or used fresh, are often spread in areas of known carp concentrations prior to making a seine haul during the warmer months of the year. Hoop-net fishermen also frequently tie bags of ground grain, soybean cakes, or alfalfa pellets in their nets during the summer to increase their harvest of carp.

When the seine's wings have been pulled to shore, the central bag, or pocket, of the net is suspended between boats and the fish are removed. (Courtesy, Illinois Natural History Survey.)

Utilization of Carp in North America

The status of carp in the United States and Canada is very different from that in other countries. Throughout Europe and Asia, the carp is an important and widely cultured food fish. For centuries, Asians have held the carp in high esteem. Revered as a noble and honorable fish, the carp has been a frequent subject of Japanese and Chinese art and culture, and selectively bred as a beautiful animal to display in oriental garden ponds. In some European countries, England for example, the carp is also considered an excellent sport species, being ranked almost on a par with trout and salmon. Fishing clubs devoted to the conservation and propagation of carp for sport angling are commonplace throughout Europe.

Most persons in North America consider the carp as nothing more than a destructive and undesirable fish. The consumption of carp as table food has been confined primarily either to local areas where they are harvested commercially, or to large cities where ethnic groups have historically accepted carp as a good food fish. As a result of the carp's general lack of acceptance, which has depressed its harvest and utilization over the years, the maximum benefits of this species have never been fully realized. To comprehend why the carp never attained a desirable status in the United States and Canada, one must examine the many interrelated and complex social, environmental, and economic changes that have occurred since its introduction.

Following the rapid population explosion and development of commercial carp fisheries within the waters of southern Canada and the United States during the

Gill nets are long stationary curtains of coarse netting. Carp try to swim through mesh openings that are large enough for their heads but too small for their bodies. They become snagged by their gill covers or fins. (Courtesy, Illinois Department of Conservation.)

late 1800s and early 1900s, good markets for this fish were quickly established. European and Asian immigrants knew that the carp was a good food fish because their traditions involved eating them. The preparation of special fish dishes such as "gefilte fish" during certain religious festivals and holidays, and religious practices of eating fish on a specific day of the week, made buying fish commonplace. This was also the period when street vendors, who purchased the surplus or less marketable-sized fish from the central markets, would peddle such species as carp on the streets of New York, Boston, Philadelphia, Toronto, Chicago, St. Louis, San Francisco and other cities. This led to carp becoming known as "fish of the masses" or "poor man's fish."

However, carp were not sold only to those of foreign ancestry, certain religious groups, or poor people. Many of the prominent hotels and restaurants also purchased carp. Restaurants of the Waldorf and Astoria hotels in New York City listed on their menu "Carp in Rhine Wine Sauce" for about 50 cents, along with such fishes as bluegill, mackerel, kingfish, halibut, and weakfish for the same or slightly lower price. The carp was an abundant, cheap, and popular food fish, and the sale of this fish continued to increase during the early 1900s.

The first indications that carp were losing favor in North America became evident even before the turn of the century. Some fish culturists who first attempted to raise carp in their ponds became quickly disillusioned because they were unable to make a profit from such a venture. Poorly constructed ponds of

Once a gill net laden with carp has been lifted into the boat, the job of extracting the fish can be long and tedious. (Courtesy, Illinois Department of Conservation.)

Gill-net fishing for carp under the ice can be productive but uncomfortable. (Courtesy, Illinois Department of Conservation.)

inadequate depth often resulted in poor water quality leading to poor survival, or the fish escaped due to dam overflows or washouts. Some customers of that time became disenchanted with carp because the species was not as palatable as many native fishes. Some diners objected to the numerous small bones in carp flesh and to the muddy or weedy flavor sometimes encountered.

As the carp became dominant in many lakes and rivers, they were blamed for destroying the nests or eating the eggs and young of more desirable native fishes. Many fishermen and hunters developed a passionate dislike for carp, accusing them of rooting out beds of aquatic vegetation. This habitat was considered essential for the spawning of some fishes, the protection of young fishes, and the production of food for waterfowl. Some hunters even accused carp of eating small ducklings.

Other persons became so convinced that carp would cause the loss of all native fishes that a bounty of one dollar was proposed for every carp killed. However, fish managers who were familiar with the carp's high reproductive potential, and with its ability to adapt to a variety of aquatic habitats and differing water quality, were aware of the folly of such a notion. They were soon to declare that the carp was here to stay, and that the best management was to harvest carp heavily and use them to feed the nation's rapidly expanding human population. It was during this same period that members of the American Fisheries Society first questioned the carp's negative impact on production of largemouth and smallmouth bass. It was concluded that bass were capable of defending their nests and young in spite of the presence of a large carp population.

While there is little doubt that the rapid population expansion of carp increased competition for food and space with game fishes, human alterations of the aquatic environment during the early 1900s were just as detrimental to native fishes. Thousands of acres of shallow lakes and sloughs in river bottomlands were leveed and drained, eliminating essential spawning, nursery, and feeding areas and protective cover. Rivers were being dammed for navigation. Lakes and rivers became the dumping sites for ever-increasing loads of domestic and industrial wastes created by the rapidly expanding human population. No matter what caused native fishes to decline, the carp was frequently made the scapegoat for undesirable changes. The carp's ability to survive in stagnant and polluted waters further tarnished the public's image of carp as a food fish.

Following World War II, the saltwater commercial fishing industry was able to capture a major portion of the market by consolidating and modernizing their operations. The development of larger, more efficient fishing vessels and gear resulted in tremendous production increases. Improvements in processing, packaging, storage, and shipment facilities resulted in a reduction of operational costs.

As carp move down the tunnel formed by a hoop net, they pass through one or more cone-shaped baffles that prevent the fish from returning the way they came in. (Courtesy, Illinois Natural History Survey.)

The industry also provided a great variety of fish and shellfish products. These products were boneless or deboned, individually portioned, breaded, attractively packaged, and easily prepared for consumption. These factors forced a sharp decline of sales of freshwater fish products. To further strengthen their position as the major supplier of fish products, the saltwater fish industry sought government assistance for fish and gear research and development of new products and markets, causing further deterioration of the economic stability and competitiveness of the freshwater fishing industry.

During the same period, the freshwater commercial fishing industry continued in its old ways. Little or no effort was made to modernize or to take full advantage of economic and human resources, the existing fish stocks, technological developments, and established markets to remain competitive with other meat-producing industries. Instead of providing new fish products desired by consumers, the industry continued to offer fresh and smoked fish products as before.

The culture and marketing of channel catfish in the southern region of the United States also had a negative effect on the commercial harvest and use of carp. By promoting the popularity of channel catfish as a favored tablefare, this industry also captured a substantial portion of those customers who formerly purchased carp and carp products. This was done by producing a large, year-round supply of the sizes of fish having uniform flesh and taste characteristics desired by consumers. Further, many consumers switched to eating pond-reared fishes because of their fear that fishes caught from natural waters could be chemically contaminated.

Although substantial progress has been made in reducing the kinds and amounts of pollutants being dumped into the waters of North America, chemical contamination of fishes is still a problem in some areas. Even when use of persistent, highly toxic chemicals has been banned for years, these chemicals still show up in the flesh of some fishes at concentrations exceeding Food and Drug Administration permissible levels. The effect on the commercial fishing industry has often been disastrous. In some cases, entire commercial fisheries have been closed; in other instances, the harvest of only one or two species is permitted. In still other situations, various pollutants have caused taste and odor problems, further reducing sales of commercial species.

The utilization of carp also decreased because of new products introduced by agricultural industries. By taking full advantage of the latest animal husbandry technology, farmers have greatly increased their efficiency of producing beef, pork, chicken, and turkey. Since most North Americans prefer poultry and red meats over fish, and because a wide variety of these products are available at competitive prices, neither the freshwater nor the saltwater fish industry has made any significant inroads into the markets of major meat producers.

Widespread public opposition to commercial fishing over the years has also had an important impact on the commercial harvest of carp and some other species. Even before the turn of the century, many people opposed the use of drag seines in natural waters because they believed that seines destroyed the nests of fish or killed young fish. Other persons sought a ban on the use of trammel nets, gill nets, and hoop nets during the spring because they caught adult fishes as they attempted to reach their spawning ground. Many people opposed these nets on the basis that they were too efficient. They believed that millions of pounds of fish were wasted, because all that were caught could not be sold. Some persons thought that any fish caught in these nets surely would die even if released. Others were convinced that commercial fishermen held little regard for the welfare of the fishery resource and would take any and all fish that might be marketed, whether legally or illegally. Such public opinion resulted in the imposition of more restrictive fishing seasons and limits on size and species of fish to be taken commercially. In extreme cases, commercial fishing was banned altogether.

Over the past 50 years, other developments have affected commercial fishing and thus the harvest and utilization of carp. As sportfishing grew by leaps and bounds, agencies expanded fish management programs to meet demands for more and better sportfishing. Where less valuable commercial fishes dominated some waters, their reduction or elimination was deemed essential to restoration of quality angling for many sport fishes. To promote these rehabilitation programs, fishery management agencies often described commercial fishes as being rough, trash or junk fish, further eroding acceptance by the public. Within the past 25 years, the stocking of large trophy fishes, such as muskellunge, striped bass, and their hybrids, has also had a major impact on commercial fishing in many states. Frequently, where fishable populations of these trophy species were established, the opposition of sport fishermen and some fishery management agencies resulted in the elimination or reduction of commercial fishing, forcing many fishermen and fish markets out of business.

It is quite amazing that a freshwater commercial fishery has even managed to survive to the present time, considering the social prejudices against this industry and the continuing degradation of the environment. Whether or not a future exists for this fishery depends on both changes in the industry and changes in attitudes of the consumer and the sport fishing fraternity. Despite their decline in popularity, carp are still being harvested and consumed by millions of people throughout North America.

References

Anderson, A. W., et al. 1949. Fishery statistics of the United States, 1945. U.S. Fish and Wildlife Service, Bureau of Commercial Fisheries, Statistical Digest 18.

Anderson, A. W., et al. 1953. Fishery statistics of the United States, 1950. U.S. Fish and Wildlife Service, Bureau of Commercial Fisheries, Statistical Digest 27.

Anderson, A. W., et al. 1957. Fishery statistics of the United States, 1955. U.S. Fish and Wildlife Service, Bureau of Commercial Fisheries, Statistical Digest 41.

Baldwin, N. S., R. W. Saalfeld, M. A. Ross, and H. J. Buettner. 1979. Commercial fish production in the Great Lakes, 1867–1977. Great Lakes Fishery Commission Technical Report 3 (1979 edition).

Cole, L. J. 1905. The German carp in the United States. *In* Report of the Bureau of Fisheries, 1904. U.S. Department of Commerce and Labor, Bureau of Fisheries, Washington, D.C.

Fielder, R. H. 1932. Fisheries industries of the United States. Appendix III *in* Report of the Commissioners of Fisheries for the fiscal year 1930. U.S. Department of Commerce, Washington, D.C.

Fielder, R. H. 1933. Fisheries industries of the United States. Appendix III *in* Report of the Commissioners of Fisheries for the fiscal year 1933. U.S. Department of Commerce, Washington, D.C.

Fielder, R. H. 1938. Fisheries industries of the United States. Appendix II *in* Report of the Commissioners of Fisheries for the fiscal year 1935. U.S. Department of Commerce, Washington, D.C.

Fielder, R. H. 1943. Fisheries statistics of the United States, 1940. U.S. Fish and Wildlife Service. Bureau of Commercial Fisheries, Statistical Digest 4.

Great Lakes Fishery Commission. 1982–1983. Annual reports for the years 1978–1981. Ann Arbor, Michigan.

Illinois State Fish Commission. 1884. Report of the board to the Governor of Illinois, 30 September 1884. Springfield, Illinois.

Illinois State Fish Commission. 1886. Report of the board to the Governor of Illinois, 30 September 1886. Springfield, Illinois.

Illinois State Fish Commission. 1891. Report of the board to the Governor of Illinois, 30 September 1891. Springfield, Illinois.

Illinois State Fish Commission. 1897. Report of the board to the Governor of Illinois, 1 October 1894 to 30 September 1896. Springfield, Illinois.

Illinois State Fish Commission. 1899. Report of the board to the Governor of Illinois, 1 October 1896 to 30 September 1898. Springfield, Illinois.

Illinois State Fish Commission. 1901. Report of the commissioners from 1 October 1898 to 30 September 1900. Springfield, Illinois.

Lyles, C. H. 1967. Fishery statistics of the United States, 1965. U.S. Fish and Wildlife Service, Bureau of Commercial Fisheries, Statistical Digest.

Power, E. A. 1960–1964. Fishery statistics of the United States. U.S. Fish and Wildlife Service, Bureau of Commercial Fisheries, Statistical Digest.

Smiley, C. W. 1883. The German carp and its introduction in the United States. U.S. Fish Commission Bulletin 3.

Smiley, C. W. 1886. Some results of carp culture in the United States. Report of the U.S. Fish Commission, 1884. Washington, D.C.

Smith, H. M. 1894. The fyke nets and fyke net fisheries of the United States, with notes on the fyke nets of other countries. U.S. Fish Commission Bulletin 12.

Smith, H. M. 1895. A statistical report on the fisheries of the Middle Atlantic States. U.S. Fish Commission Bulletin 14.

Smith, H. M. 1897. Report of the Commissioner for the year ending 1895. U.S. Commission of Fish and Fisheries, Washington, D.C.

Smith, H. M. 1898. Statistics of the fisheries of the interior waters of the United States. Report of the Commissioner for the year ending 30 June 1896, part 12. U.S. Commission of Fish and Fisheries, Washington, D.C.

U.S. Commission of Fish and Fisheries. 1879. Report of the Commissioner for 1877, part 5. Washington, D.C.

U.S. Commission of Fish and Fisheries. 1884. Report of the Commissioner for 1882. part 10. Washington, D.C.

U.S. Department of Commerce. 1911. Fisheries of the United States, 1908. Washington, D.C.

U.S. Fish Commission. 1874. Report of the Commissioner for 1872 and 1873. Washington, D.C.

U.S. Fish Commission. 1876. Report of the Commissioner for 1873 and 1874, 1874 and 1875. Washington, D.C.

U.S. Fish Commission. 1879. Report of the Commissioner for 1877. Washington, D.C.

U.S. Fish Commission. 1882–1885. U.S. Fish Commission Bulletins 2–5. Washington, D.C.

U.S. Fish Commission. 1887. U.S. Fish Commission Bulletin 7. Washington, D.C.

U.S. National Marine Fisheries Service. [No date.] Fisheries statistics of the United States, 1967–1977. Washington, D.C.

Sport Fishing for Carp

RONALD J. SPITLER

The common carp acquired a bad reputation soon after its introduction to North American waters in the late 1800s. Imported as a food fish, carp acclimated so successfully that it soon became a trash fish, especially in habitats managed for waterfowl or warmwater fishes. As a fishery biologist, I recently helped to destroy 2 million pounds of carp in 1 year under an approved fishery management plan. But if it were not for the carp, I might never have become a fishery biologist, or have been hooked on sportfishing.

Where I grew up in Ohio, small panfish and bullheads offered the best chances for fishing success, as was true in many places. The occasional big fish that I caught was a carp, fishing with my neighbor Tom Flick in the "Old Mill Stream." I have fond and vivid memories of big carp pulling against the frail lightweight rod and 6-pound-test line that we used. We lost more fish than we landed, but I remember that the thrill of catching a large carp was, to me, equal to that of catching bass or other game fish.

Fortunately, many North American anglers are becoming aware of the good qualities of carp. They are tremendous fighters on light fishing tackle, their eating quality equals salmon when smoked, and they are as palatable as most fishes when properly dressed and cooked. Many persons have been pleasantly surprised at how good carp are to eat, when they were not prejudiced beforehand by tales of this "foul-tasting fish." If you are not now an experienced carp angler, perhaps this book will pique your curiosity enough to find out for yourself if you are missing some good fishing and eating.

Public Attitudes Toward Carp

Worldwide, more carp are cultured for food than any other fish. But were you aware that, in Europe, carp ranks third among all sport fishes, surpassed only by Atlantic salmon and rainbow trout? European anglers who fish for carp preach and practice the philosophy of catch and release. Their ideals and methods are very similar to those held by members of Trout Unlimited and the Bass Angler's Sportsman's Society in North America. Although carp fishing contests are not held, publications by carp angler's organizations include many photographs of proud anglers holding "twenties" (20 pounds plus) and "thirties" (30 pounds plus) prior to releasing them. The British Carp Angler's Association has detailed records of individual carp being caught 300–500 times during their lifetimes.

The equipment and fishing methods of a dedicated European carp angler rank among the most interesting and complex, rivaling those of salmon and trout anglers. Ten-foot rods with spinning reels are typical, and special rod holders,

Roger Smith returning a 33-pound mirror carp to an English water. Carp are raised commercially for the table in England, but carp anglers release all the fish they catch. (Courtesy, Tim Paisley.)

unique bite indicators, and careful fishing presentations are common, plus an amazing array of baits.

A sharp contrast exists in fishing waters as well. In England, carp waters are widespread and many are stocked. Some lakes are managed exclusively for larger carp (10 pounds or more). More importantly, on popular waters it is not unusual for the same fish to be caught and released 20 to 30 times per season, necessitating some very shrewd baits and methods to recapture what fisheries biologists consider to be one of the smartest of fish. In North America, carp are much more easily caught by anglers, and are generally of larger average size than in Europe, as witnessed by the state records listed at the end of this chapter.

There has been a rediscovery of carp by many anglers in North America and the carp, as a sport fish, is slowly making a comeback. As evidence, some information in this chapter came from the *Carp Newsletter Quarterly* published in Pleasant Valley, Wisconsin.

Fishing Equipment

Perhaps a brief description of what happens when a large carp is hooked will help you determine what type of equipment to use. Carp are powerful fish, typically making long, seemingly tireless runs, much like chinook salmon. If they are in weedy or brushy waters, they will surely entangle themselves and the line.

With that in mind, select a medium-action rod with progressive taper, at least 6 feet long. The longer the rod (up to 11 feet) the better the chances of successfully handling a large fish. A good quality fiberglass rod will suffice. Choose a medium-weight, open-face spinning reel possessing a good drag and capable of holding 120 yards of 12-pound-test line. A spin-casting reel can be used so long as it has sufficient line capacity and an excellent drag system. Some bait-casting reels have anti-reverse overrides on them, but they may provide too much resistance to the pull of the line when a fish starts to run. Carp will likely drop a bait at the first hint of resistance. Hooks should be strong so they will not bend or straighten easily, single or treble pointed, and sharp. Size numbers two through six are most suitable. They should be tied directly on the line with a good knot.

The line should be of good quality monofilament or braided, and may range from 8- to 12-pound test. Lighter or heavier lines will be dictated by the fishing conditions and angler expectations. Ultralight tackle may provide a great deal of fun and success in open lake fishing, but would be useless in water full of aquatic weeds or snags.

Quill bobbers may be useful under certain circumstances, but you should avoid the ball-shaped floats since they offer too much resistance to a biting carp. Sinkers may be necessary, so have on hand an assortment of small split shot, slip sinkers, egg sinkers, and common bell sinkers of ⅛ to ½ ounce. Snaps and swivels, not recommended as end connectors to the hooks, are nonetheless useful as sinker stops or slides under certain conditions. A sturdy landing net is desirable. Bite indicators, quite common in Europe, can be helpful on tough fishing days. These and other specialized gear will be discussed as they apply to each method.

Tim Paisley with an English leather carp of over 30 pounds. This fish usually is caught two or three times each season. Some carp become so well known that they are given individual names by English anglers. (Courtesy, Tim Paisley.)

Fishing Methods

The common method of carp fishing has changed little over the years in North America. It is indistinguishable from other bait-fishing techniques except for the types of baits often used. Typically, the carp angler uses doughballs made of various grains, sweeteners, and flour; whole-kernel corn; or earthworms for bait. She ties a medium to large hook on 10- to 20-pound-test monofilament line complete with ½-ounce sinker, then casts the bait to a likely looking spot some distance from shore. Tightening the line to remove all slack, she braces the rod, handle down, against a nearby rock or forked tree branch stuck into the ground. When carp are actively feeding, the usual bite is an obvious grab and run. The angler quickly sets the hook and lands the fish if she is lucky. On days when carp are less active, their biting may be much less noticeable. In fact, it is not at all unusual for the angler to reel in her line only to find a bare hook. On such days the catch rate is very low.

By contrast, the English have advanced carp fishing almost to a science. A typical carp fishing trip in England may involve weeks of planning and preparation. The angler carefully prepares his favorite bait, a high-protein type (60% protein or more), or a boiled bait mixed with eggs, locally called "boiles." If the selected water is not far from home, he may prebait the water several times. Such chumming not only attracts more carp to the fishing area, but allows them to develop a taste for the bait that later will have hooks in it.

Finally, the angler will drive to the lake, pond, or pit, carry his gear and food to the cleared fishing spot, called a swim, and literally set up camp. If he is a serious angler, he will have his bed chair, which looks like a lounge chair with separately adjustable legs and tilts back for sitting or sleeping, a sleeping bag, rain gear, beach umbrella for shade and shelter, and perhaps even a tent, called a brollywrap, that fits over the umbrella and bed chair. Once set up, the fisherman will prebait the swim one more time, bait up his two specialized rods, cast his offerings to likely carp holding locations, place his rods in their holders, attach bite indicators, then sit back and relax. While he enjoys his 1- to 3-day vigil, he hopes not to be bothered by competition from anglers fishing for small fish, called maggot mashers, or inexperienced carp anglers, called noddys.

In contrast to the typical American fishing outfit, the English prefer longer rods, usually in the 10- to 11-foot range. According to Peter Mohan, founder of the British Carp Study Group, the longer rods facilitate easy casts to great distances while allowing quick line pickups for powerful hook sets, and provide good backbone to subdue large carp. In North America, we have many suppliers of such rods, but they are usually for salmon and steelhead fishing.

Anglers in England use two rod rests per rod, adjusted so that the rod tip points downward at the water, providing least resistance to biting carp. Coupled with this, almost a necessity, are bite indicators to show that a fish has taken the bait. They range from a piece of foil or paper draped over the line to rather elaborate electric bite indicators. It is important to have a gap in the rod rest under the rod for the line to slip through easily.

Perhaps the easiest and best indicator is of American origin—a small chunk of styrofoam, such as the bottom of a coffee cup, slit with a knife to accept the line. This flag is clipped lightly to the line immediately in front of the reel. To make it

The camp of an English carp angler who is set up for a long session. (Courtesy, Tim Paisley.)

even more sensitive, enough line is pulled off the reel to allow the indicator to lie on the ground. This "flag" is attached to a short piece of line tied to the rear rod support so that once a good bite occurs and the hook is set, the indicator does not fly off and litter the area.

Bite indicators are especially useful on windy days. Old umbrella spokes or welding rods may be used as needles, set in the ground at an angle, to hold tubular indicators in windy conditions. A biting carp will slide the indicators up and off the needles. Be sure to leave the reel free-running so that you do not lose your rod from a quick run of a 10-pound carp.

Lake and Pond Fishing

There always seems to be a best time to fish. Sunrise to late morning is consistently the ideal time to go for carp in summer. The next best period seems to be late in the day, up to sundown. Of course, carp may be caught at all hours of the day and night, so go when you can.

Assume that you have picked your fishing lake or pond based on advice of friends, the local bait shop, or your nearest natural resources agency; how do you then proceed? Select your fishing location carefully. Carp concentrations will usually be found in the shallower portions of lakes or ponds, in bays. Pick a spot where you can comfortably fish from a shoreline that is relatively free of snags or heavy weeds. Scattered weed beds within casting range are desirable, especially floating vegetation such as water lilies. Fishing from a boat may be satisfactory at times, but this complicates your ability to sense a bite in choppy waters.

A carp rod double-mounted in the English style. Note the simple bite indicator consisting of a ring slipped over a stick. (Drawn by John Cooper.)

If chumming or groundbaiting is legal in your area, toss a handful of the bait into the fishing spot immediately upon arriving and periodically while fishing. Better yet, chum the area daily for at least 3 days prior to fishing. Carp can be trained in this manner to be more receptive to your offering. Not only that, instead of a few scattered fish to angle for, a properly chummed area may have a concentration of many carp waiting for your tidbit. Just hit the area daily with the same bait.

At the end of this chapter, you will find a list of baits and recipes. Only a few will be discussed here because of the special techniques required in the situations where they are best used. For now, let us assume that canned whole kernel corn is the best carp bait.

To fish the spot, simply put from one to several kernels of corn on the hook and cast to the chummed area. If long casts are desired, use a slip sinker away from the hook; tie a barrel swivel 6 to 8 inches above the hook, and have the sinker above the swivel. If the bottom is very soft, consider using a standard bell sinker on a 6-inch dropper tied to a snap or swivel placed above the barrel swivel. This too will slip on the line, but will not pull the bait into a soft bottom.

Place your rod on the rod holders, take up the slack line, and hook up the bite indicator if you choose to use one. The indicator is most useful on windy days; otherwise, you may want to leave slack line out and become a line watcher.

When the line starts to move, indicating a carp run, set the hook, hard. Most of the time, carp will pick up the bait, sometimes after mouthing it for a couple of minutes, and start to move off. Once you notice your line moving steadily away, you know where the hook is. Few such bites are missed.

When bobbers are used, the quill type is the most desirable since it offers the least resistance to biting carp. If one is used, the double rod holder and bite indicators are not necessary; just watch the bobber instead. Keep the bait near, or on, the bottom. Take up as much slack line as possible before setting the hook.

On occasion, and especially in early morning, you may observe carp feeding on debris at the surface. The English call this "clooping" because of the sucking sound made by the fish. Surface fishing can be exciting, as any bass angler will tell you. When carp are feeding on the surface, the best bait is a piece of bread with its crust intact. Take an uncut loaf of bread, cut a piece from it of ½ to 1 ½ inches square, leaving the crust unbroken. Pinch the soft part of the bread hard, and insert the hook through the crust from the top. Carefully cast this to the "cloopers." Do not set the hook until you are certain a fish has taken it and has started moving away.

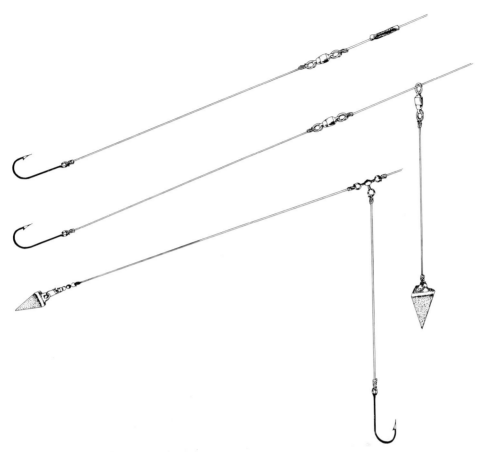

Three ways of mounting hooks and sinkers on carp-fishing lines. (Drawn by John Cooper.)

When everything but carp consistently takes your bait, you might want to try a half-boiled potato. Use one about the size of a golf ball, with just a hook, no sinker. Small fish cannot break it apart so they do not bother it. After you have chummed an area a few days, you will find that the carp have adjusted favorably to this new food.

Night Fishing

Fishing at night can bring many rewards. It is usually quieter, there are fewer disturbances from other anglers and especially boaters, and it produces fish. Many anglers profess nighttime to be the best time for taking big fish. You can be the judge of that through your own experience. The best time is just before daybreak, but action can come at any time after sundown.

Fish the same familiar waters as in daytime and fish in the same manner, except that bobbers should not be used. Dress warmly, take plenty of insect repellent along, and do not forget a flashlight. Ardent carp anglers suggest not using lights unless absolutely necessary. Carp may be closer to shore after dark so it is a good idea to fish at least one bait near shore.

This brings us to a novel and exciting English technique, that of fishing the "margin patrol," made up of shallow-swimming, actively feeding carp. In margin fishing, you will want to fish the windblown shoreline, where drifting food collects. You must be quiet and without lights of any kind. Place a small piece of bread crust on a sharp hook, crumb side down. Place a rod rest so that the tip of your rod hangs just over the water's edge and lower the crust until it just enters the water so that no line is actually in the water. Pull some slack line off the reel and let it lie on the ground, as a precaution against a surprise strike separating you from your equipment. A mixture of bread crumbs and water can be poured into the water as an additional attractant. If you get a bite, the carp will either take the bread crust so quietly as to amaze you, or the water will suddenly explode, and so will you. The slack line will allow the carp to take the bait, and once the line and fish are going, set the hook. This exciting close-in fishing in darkness is not for the faint at heart!

Bite indicators, especially the electronic buzzer types are valuable under night-time conditions. Lighted indicators are also available. If you are using monofilament line, a novel but effective way to watch your line without spooking fish or lighting up a large area is to purchase a black light (ultraviolet). When it is turned on in the darkness, it makes monofilament glow like a neon tube.

Lacking bite indicators or an appropriate light source, you can expect to miss a few bites, so check your bait more frequently than during the daytime. Be prepared for a good deal of suspense once you set the hook, because you probably

Good carp fishing is available on slow-moving waters over most of North America. (Courtesy, Kansas Fish and Game Commission.)

will not be able to judge distance from shore, or size, or even species of fish until you get it to the net.

River Angling

Fishing for carp in moving water can present an exciting challenge, especially if there is a strong current, many snags, and possibly a hole or two that could float a wading angler's hat if he or she is not careful. Or, it can be quite similar to lake fishing if there is only a slight current.

My most exciting fishing for carp was in the Blanchard River, in Ohio, below a dam. Here a hooked fish invariably headed downstream with the current, using it to its advantage. To keep the bait where the angler wants it in a current, more weight is required than in a lake, and it may be desirable to reverse the position of the bait and sinker. Both items must be securely fastened to the line with the hook on a dropper. In this manner the bait will be just off the bottom while the sinker may be resting against or under a snag on the bottom.

River anglers often change their method of fishing by using a bobber in order to let the bait drift slowly downstream. To do this, simply add a few split shot 6 to 8 inches above the bait, to keep it near the bottom, then add a quill bobber at least a foot or two further upline from the bait than the stream depth. For example, in a 3-foot-deep stream area, set the bobber 4 to 5 feet above the bait. The bobber will not only help avoid snags on the bottom, but will provide a good signal when a carp stops the bait and moves off with it. Careful adjustment of the split shot may be necessary to get the proper drift.

Artificial Flies and Lures

When it comes to fly-fishing we are drifting a bit into the unknown, since information on the use of this technique for carp is scarce. Many carp anglers use fly rods but they fish them with the usual carp baits. Since we know that carp are occasionally caught on artificial lures and that they eat almost anything, let's discuss some "what ifs." What if a fly angler approached some "clooping" carp and presented a nice juicy-looking dry fly right in front of them? What if a slow sinking nymph were cast into an area of cruising or bottom-feeding carp? What if a wet fly resembling a crayfish were drifted through a pool of carp in a stream known to have crayfish? Give it a try; it probably is easier to do than you imagine. Be very quiet and deliberate as you stalk your prey, and use medium to heavy fly-fishing equipment and a fairly heavy tippet. Dull colored clothing, even camouflage, may be helpful.

I have often caught carp on artificial lures, especially jigs. Carp can also be caught on crank baits, spoons, spinners, and especially on soft plastic worms and grubs. To take carp consistently on artificial lures may be difficult, but it can be fun, particularly on those restless days when it is difficult to sit and wait for the fish. Just as in fly-fishing, find the carp activity and match the hatch as best you can.

Bow-fishing and Spearing

Bow-and-arrow fishing for carp can provide a great deal of challenge and action. A bow having a draw strength of 30 pounds or more is necessary since those big carp scales seem like armor plating at times. The reel can be purchased, or it might be as simple as a 1-pound coffee can secured to a narrow board that is, in turn,

Bow hunting for carp in Kansas. (Courtesy, Kansas Fish and Game Commission.)

taped to the bow, or it can be a spin-casting reel attached in a similar manner. Buy a good quality fish arrow, keep the point sharp, and use 30 to 50 feet of heavy line (80- to 100-pound test).

The easiest bow-fishing is at spawning time, which is late spring to early summer. The carp are less wary then and usually in water shallow enough to be easily seen. Wear a hat and polarized sunglasses, not only to see fish better but to protect your eyes and face from strong reflected sunlight on bright days. When shooting, be very careful to keep the line clear of your wristwatch, clothing, buttons, and bow projections.

Once spawning is over, the carp can still be found in good numbers in shallow bays. You may use a small, stable boat, or wade. But remember that the stalk is very important and that you are dealing with one of the wariest fish known. Some personal observations convinced me of this fact.

I was bow-fishing in a shallow flat at the western end of Lake Erie and could see thousands of carp feeding. Thinking that the biggest ones were farther from shore, I figured that I could wade carefully through the closer concentration of carp, then take my pick of the big ones. I had not taken more than a few steps when I accidently touched a carp with my boot. All of a sudden the water around me exploded as, like falling dominoes, the carp moved away from me into deeper water. Never had I seen such a sight. It was like a stampeding herd of cattle. In a matter of a minute or so, I was very much alone in acres of water. It was nearly a half-hour later before I even saw another carp.

During the summertime, carp are not as easy a quarry when they are in deeper and clearer water. It is important to compensate for light refraction when aiming at a fish. If the back of your target is not projecting above the surface, aim under the fish. In deeper water, aim even further below it. Otherwise you will surely miss and scare the fish away.

Little can be said for spearing that has not already been said about bow-fishing. Use a stout spear with sharp tines and, as with bow-fishing, be sure your quarry

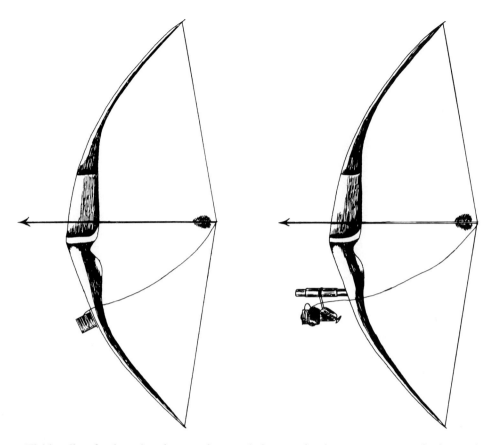

Fishing line for bow hunting can be spooled on a simple core or on a spinning reel attached to the bow. (Drawn by John Cooper.)

is what you think it is before killing it. Spearing and bow-fishing may be prohibited in some states. Be sure to check on the rules governing your area before setting out to do either.

Carp-Fishing Waters

Wherever you live, there is a good chance you will discover carp-fishing spots nearby. Inquire of your local bait and tackle shops, other anglers, or your nearest natural resources office. There may also be places for fee fishing or specially stocked ponds. If contacts with your state agency indicate that there are no such waters nearby, perhaps you may want to request that a carp fishing program be started.

Throughout North America, there are urban fishing programs where carp are, or may be, stocked to improve fishing opportunities. Additionally, there are many fee-fishing waters, especially those stocked with catfish, where carp may now be or could be included. The potential for expanding such fishing for a truly quality fish is tremendous.

A list at the end of this chapter includes the three best carp fishing waters in 35 states and 6 Canadian provinces. This information was provided from a questionnaire sent to all states and provinces. If your state or province is not included, it

Spearfishing for carp can be good sport where the water is clear. (Courtesy, Missouri Department of Conservation.)

probably does not have good carp fishing waters. Approximate locations in the states or provinces are in parentheses.

References

Anonymous. [No date.] Hook 'n cook carp. Pamphlet of the Manitoba Department of Mines, Natural Resources and Environment, Winnipeg, Manitoba, Canada. 4 p.

Anonymous. 1936. The carp has a future. Michigan Conservation 5(11):2, 11.

Atta, E. L. 1965. Carp at their best. Pennsylvania Angler 34(5):24–25.

Bartlett, S. P. 1903. Angling for carp and some hints as to the best mode of cooking. Transactions of the American Fisheries Society 32:47–50.

Bartlett, S. P. 1905. Carp, as seen by a friend. Transactions of the American Fisheries Society 34:207–216.

Bartlett, S. P. 1910. The future of the carp. Transactions of the American Fisheries Society 39:151–154.

Black, J. D. 1944. "Carp problem" in 1901. Wisconsin Conservation Bulletin 9(7):6.

Brown, K. [No date.] The Ken Brown guide to bowfishing. Ken Brown Publications, Hugo, Oklahoma.

Burnside, T. R. 1957. Carp fishing at night. Carp Newsletter Quarterly 2(1):7–8. (Pleasant Valley, Wisconsin.)

Byam, W. R. [No date.] Fun unlimited: carp fishing. Wisconsin Conservation Bulletin 22(6):10–13.

Cole, L. J. 1905. The status of the carp in America. Transactions of the American Fisheries Society 34:201–206.

Gapen, D. D. 1973. Why fish carp? Dan Gapen, Big Lake, Minnesota. 46 p.

Hekkers, J. [No date.] Carp. Twenty million Europeans can't all be wrong. Bulletin of the Colorado Division of Wildlife, Denver, Colorado.

Hiller, I. 1980. Consider the carp. Bulletin of the Texas Parks and Wildlife Department, Austin, Texas.

Hilton, J. 1972. Quest for carp. Pelham Books, London, England.

Hunt, W. T. 1911. As for the carp. Transactions of the American Fisheries Society 41:189–193.

Kreh, B. 1967. Secret lure for carp. Sports Afield, February:52–53.

Maddocks, K. [No date.] Carp fever. Beckay Publishers, Enfield, England. 280 p.

McCrimmon, H. R. 1968. Carp in Canada. Fisheries Research Board of Canada Bulletin 165. 93 p.

Miller, G. 1977. Let's get serious about carp! Nebraska Conservationist, June:12–16.

Miller, G. [No date.] Time out for carp. Bulletin of the Nebraska Game and Parks Commission, Lincoln, Nebraska.

Miller, N. J. 1962. Carp, anyone? Wisconsin Conservation Bulletin 27(2):22–23.

Mohan, P. 1982. Basic carp fishing. Beckay Publishers, Enfield, England. 132 p.

Mraz, D. 1954. Carp vs. largemouth bass. Wisconsin Conservation Bulletin 19(4):18–19.

Nash, N. 1959. Carp fishing. Missouri Conservationist 20(3):8–9.

Neess, J. C., et al. 1957. Some vital statistics in a heavily-exploited population of carp. Journal of Wildlife Management 21:279–292.

Peterson, E. T., and R. A. Drews. 1957. Some historical aspects of the carp with special reference to Michigan. Michigan Department of Conservation, Fish Division Pamphlet 23. 5 p.

Peterson, L. I. 1958. Improvements in carp fishing. Wisconsin Conservation Bulletin 23(6):7–11.

Potter, R. E. 1948. Minnesota carp. Conservation Volunteer 11(6):10–14.

Thomas, M. 1955. Carp . . . champ of the heavyweights. Pennsylvania Fish Commission. Pennsylvania Angler 24(8):8–9.

Angling Records for Carp

World Records

The International Game Fish Association (IGFA), through strict qualification rules, keeps tabs on world records in three categories: (1) All Tackle World Record, the heaviest fish on any line or class; (2) Line Class World Records, the heaviest fish on lines of various test strengths; and (3) Fly Rod World Records, the heaviest fish caught on tippets of various test strengths. The following lists include IGFA records as of the spring of 1985.

IGFA Freshwater All-Tackle World Record Carp.—The official IGFA world record is a carp of 57 pounds, 13 ounces, caught from the Potomac River, Washington, D.C., on 13 May 1983 by Jean E. Ward.

IGFA Freshwater Line Class Record Carp.—Each of the following entries gives line class in pounds, weight of carp in pounds–ounces, place where the fish was caught, date of catch, and angler. Line class U denotes unlimited weight. States are indicated by two-letter Postal Service abbreviations.

2	29–0	Patuxent River, MD	13 May 1983	Jean E. Ward
4	30–14	Lake Tanycomo, MO	4 April 1983	Craig Landals
6	35–8	Lake Geneva, WI	26 June 1984	Frank M. Metzke
8	40–0	Johnson Pond, NC	25 May 1983	Carlton Thornton
10	43–8	Bluestone Reservoir, WV	1 May 1976	Charles Frye, Jr.
12	28–2	Lake Traverse, SD	25 April 1976	Frank Martinek
14	15–5	Patuxent River, MD	14 May 1984	Jean E. Ward
15	26–8	Patuxent River, MD	14 May 1984	Jean E. Ward
16	33–0	Patuxent River, MD	10 May 1982	Jean E. Ward
17	37–5	Shawnee Mission Lake, KS	13 June 1984	William Nagle
20	44–0	Patuxent River, MD	22 May 1970	Jean E. Ward
25	26–2	Patuxent River, MD	14 May 1984	Jean E. Ward
30	39–0	Patuxent River, MD	20 May 1981	Jean E. Ward
36	26–4	Patuxent River, MD	14 May 1984	Jean E. Ward
40	25–0	Patuxent River, MD	24 May 1983	Jean E. Ward
U	55–5	Clearwater Lake, MN	10 July 1952	F. Ledwein

IGFA Freshwater Fly Rod World Record Carp.—Fly rod records are organized as above.

2	5–10	Newton, OH	1 June 1982	J. Donald Conover
4	5–8	Pascack Creek, NJ	14 May 1983	J. Caltabellata
8	22–7	Red River, Manitoba	11 May 1981	J. Miller

For additional information, write to the IGFA, 3000 East Las Olas Boulevard, Ft. Lauderdale, Florida 33316. Get the application form and regulations before you catch that new record carp.

State Records for Carp

Listed below on each line are the state of capture, weight of the carp in pounds–ounces, angler, location, and date.

AL	35–0	Darrin Jackson	Bear Creek	19 April 1980
AZ	42–0	G. Ramsfield	Lake Havasu	March 1979
CA	52–0	Lee Bryant	Nacimiento Lake	April 1968
CO	22–0	August Raisch	Cherry Creek Reservoir	1973
DE	45–0	Ronald Burnett	Delaware River	6 June 1976
FL	28–14	Dick Anderson	Apalachicola River	21 June 1978
GA	35–12	Donald Clark	Lake Jackson	1972
IL	42–0	C. Heinze	Kankakee River	1928
IN	38–1	Frank Drost	Lake County	1967
IA	50–0	F. Hougland	Glenwood Lake	May 1969
KS	37–5	William Nagle	Shawnee Lake	1984

KY	54–14	Ricky Vance	Licking River	13 March 1971
LA	33–0	J. E. Strange		May 1978
MD	44–6	Jimmy Lake	Morgantown Beach	28 April 1978
MA	31–8	Roger Pyzocha	Connecticut River	1983
MI	61–8	Dale France	Big Wolf Lake	18 May 1974
MN	55–5	Frank Ledwein	Clearwater Lake	10 July 1952
MS	74–0	Curtis Wade	Pelahatchie Lake	13 June 1963
MO	47–7	Elmer Henson		5 June 1974
MT	38–4	Craig Dyer	Eyrand Lake	1983
NE	33–12	Toni Baete	Farm pond	1983
NV	30–8	L. Frazier	Lake Mohave	
NH	27–0	M. Katryez	Merrimack River	April 1968
NJ	41–2	John Pisa	Delaware River	1971
NY	40–4	Paul Reichart	Lake Ontario	1983
NC	45–2	Max Lowder	Badin Lake	8 June 1974
ND	25–8	Claydean Berger	Lake Sarakawea	1984
OH	50–0	J. Holton	Paint Creek	24 May 1967
OK	32–12	Bob Penick	Lake Rush	13 May 1968
PA	52–0	George Brown	Juniata River	1962
SD	33–0	Jerome Haas	Pickerel Lake	6 May 1982
TN	42–8	Al Moore	Boone Reservoir	12 August 1956
TX	41–0		Pure Oil Lake	14 May 1972
UT	30–0	R. Merrill	Great Salt Lake Marsh	1960
VT	27–8	Robert Corbiere	Missisquoi River	1984
VA	60–0	Ben Topham	Private lake	5 July 1970
WV	30–1	Steve Mick	Buckhannon River	1975
WI	57–2	Mike Prorok	Lake Wisconsin	28 August 1966

Baits and Recipes

The particular merits and uses of canned corn, bread crust, and half-boiled potatoes have been discussed earlier. These three items are perhaps the best baits to fit a variety of fishing situations, and require little or no preparation. Many carp have been caught on live bait such as worms, minnows, and crayfish, but most other fishes like them too. Commercially prepared carp baits are available at many bait shops, and grocery stores are full of frequently used carp baits such as lunch meats, canned pet foods, canned potatoes, marshmallows, meat, cheeses, and vegetables.

The same food stores carry a tremendous variety of ingredients that are often used by carp anglers in concocting their secret doughballs. Some of those products are cornmeal, flour, cottonseed meal, wheat germ, corn germ, cereals, crackers, eggs, corn syrup, honey, cocoa, coffee, Jell-o, sugar, molasses, cinnamon, sorghum, peanut butter, onions, salt, grated cheese, powdered potatoes, beer, bourbon, vanilla, anise oil or seeds, and a host of other flavorings. If it smells and tastes good to you, the carp should like it too!

You can let your imagination be your guide, or you can follow some of the proven recipes that I have collected from many sources. As you develop your favorite doughball and vary the ingredients in your search for the ultimate bait, remember to write it down. Otherwise, how can you share it with me, and others, later.

Let's start off with a very basic recipe that worked well for me as a teenager and is versatile enough to accommodate most other ingredients and flavorings. I call it the 1-2-3 doughball.

1-2-3 Doughball

Ingredients: 1 cup sugar, 2 cups white flour, and 3 cups cornmeal. Mix the ingredients in a large bowl. Slowly add water and mix to the desired consistency. If the dough needs stiffening, add more flour and cornmeal. To thin it, add more water. Flatten the ball, wrap it in a cloth bag, and place it in boiling water for 20 minutes. Cool the dough, then put it in a plastic bag and refrigerate. To add other fillers, blend them in before cooking. For scents, knead them in after cooking, once the mixture cools enough to handle.

Cereal Variation of Doughballs

Ingredients: 1 cup each of flour, cottonseed meal, crushed bran flakes or other cereal, oatmeal, molasses, and water, plus ¼ cup of vanilla extract. Mix the cereal, oatmeal, molasses, vanilla, and water. Blend thoroughly and add this wet mixture to the cottonseed and flour mixture. Knead until the right texture is achieved.

Cheese Variation of Doughballs

Ingredients: 1 cup flour, 1 cup cornmeal, ½ cup grated parmesan cheese, 1 tablespoon sugar, sliced onion. Mix the ingredients together in a large bowl, then add enough cold water to form a thick dough. Roll into ¾-inch balls and drop into boiling water; cook until the balls float to the top. Remove balls, cool, and refrigerate. Keep wrapped or covered to prevent drying.

Potato Variation of Doughballs

Ingredients: 1 cup wheat flour, ½ cup cornmeal, 2 good sized potatoes, grated. Mix the ingredients into a paste, adding a little water if necessary. Put in a cloth bag and cook for 30 to 45 minutes. Cool and refrigerate. Pinch off individual baits to cover the hook.

Carp Waters

Alabama.—Lake Jordan (north of Montgomery), Lake Eufala (southwestern AL), Wheeler Reservoir (north-central AL).

Arizona.—Lake Mead (AZ–NV line), Roosevelt Lake (east of Phoenix), San Carlos Lake (100 miles east of Phoenix).

Arkansas.—Lower Arkansas River (southeastern AR), Green's Ferry Reservoir (north-central AR), Lake Hamilton (north-central AR).

British Columbia.—Fraser River (Vancouver), Shuswap Lake (Kamloops), Okanagan Lake (near USA border).

California.—Clear Lake (northern CA), Sacramento–San Joaquin River Delta (central CA), Colorado River (CA–AZ border).

Colorado.—Cherry Creek Reservoir (Denver), Ban Lake (35 miles northeast of Denver), Pueblo Reservoir (10 miles west of Pueblo).

Delaware.—Delaware River (New Castle), Augustine Beach (Port Penn), Broad Creek (Seaford).

Hawaii.—Wahiawa Reservoir (Oahu), Waita Reservoir (Kauai).

Idaho.—Snake River impoundments (southwestern ID), Lake Lowell (southwestern ID), Blackfoot Reservoir (southeastern ID).

Illinois.—Grass Lake (Lake County), Fox River (McHenry Dam, McHenry County), Carlyle Lake (Clinton, Bond, Fayette counties).

Indiana.—White River (Indianapolis), Mansfield Reservoir (Rockville), Eagle Creek Reservoir (Indianapolis).

Iowa.—Mississippi River, Des Moines River, Iowa–Cedar rivers.

Kansas.—John Redmond Reservoir (southeastern KS), Turtle Creek Reservoir (northeastern KS), Milford Reservoir (north-central KS).

Kentucky.—Kentucky Lake (western KY), Ohio River (northern KY), Barren Lake (south-central KY).

Maine.—Kennebec River (below Augusta Dam), Androscoggin River (Merrymeeting Bay vicinity), Scarboro Marsh (Scarboro).

Manitoba.—Red and Assiniboine rivers (Winnipeg), Whitemud River (Lake Manitoba), Waterhen River (Lake Winnipegosis to Lake Manitoba).

Maryland and the District of Columbia.—Potomac River (DC), Middle River (Baltimore), Susquehanna River flats (Havre de Grace), catwalk off Conowingo Dam (head of Chesapeake Bay).

Massachusetts.—Charles River (Boston), Merrimack River (Haverhill to border), Taunton River (Face River).

Michigan.—Saginaw Bay (Lake Huron), lower Grand River (Grand Haven), lower Huron River and Erie Marshes (Lake Erie).

Minnesota.—Mississippi River (Coon Rapids to Hastings), Lake Minnetonka (west of Minneapolis), Minneapolis–St. Paul area (shallow streams).

Mississippi.—Pickwick Lake (northeastern MS), all delta lakes.

Missouri.—Lake Ozark (central MO), Table Rock Lake (southwestern MO), Stockton Lake (southwestern MO).

Nevada.—Lahontan Reservoir and valley (Fallon), Washoe Lake (between Reno and Carson City), Lake Mohave (Las Vegas).

New Hampshire.—Merrimack River (Manchester to state line), Connecticut River (Wilder to state line), Mascoma Lake (Enfield).

New Mexico.—Ute Lake (Logan), McMillan Lake (Carlsbad), Conchas Lake (Tucumcari).

New York.—Lake Erie, Chautauqua Lake (western NY), Lake Champlain (VT border).

North Carolina.—Badin Lake (Charlotte), Lake Tillery (Charlotte), Jordan Reservoir (Raleigh).

Ohio.—Lake Erie (western basin), large rivers, Grand Lake Saint Marys (Salina), Buckeye Lake (Hebron), Portage Lakes (Akron).

Ontario.—Grand River, Lake St. Clair, Long Point Bay (Lake Erie).

Oregon.—Willamette River backwaters (northwestern OR), Columbia River backwaters (northern OR), Snake River impoundments (northeastern OR).

Pennsylvania.—Pymatuning Reservoir (Crawford County), lower Susquehanna River (Harrisburg to MD line), Allegheny River (below Parker).

Quebec.—St. Lawrence River, Outaouais River.

Rhode Island.—Woonasquatucket River (Johnston, near Providence), Pawtuxet River (Cranston, near Providence).

Saskatchewan.—Pasqua Lake, Mission Lake, Katepwa Lake.

South Dakota.—Missouri River reservoirs, Big Stone Lake, Lake Poinsett.

Tennessee.—Any reservoir and stream.

Utah.—Utah Lake (40 miles south of Salt Lake City), Jordan River (outflow from Utah Lake), Willard Bay Reservoir and marshes (15 miles north of Ogden).

Vermont.—Lake Champlain, Connecticut River.

West Virginia.—Ohio River (western border), Monongahela River (Marion, Monongahela counties), Kanawha River.

Wisconsin.—Lake Koshkonong (southeastern WI), Rock River (southeastern WI), Mississippi and Wisconsin rivers (western and southwestern WI).

Wyoming.—Pathfinder Reservoir (35 miles south of Casper), Boysen Reservoir (Shoshoni), Ocean Lake (Pavillion).

Eating Carp

VERN HACKER

Yes, carp are really good to eat. And, there are cooks who know how to prepare carp to make its nutritious protein into a tasty dish. If you are a skeptic, you should try carp using one or more of the tasty recipes given later.

The carp has been one of the preferred food fishes of millions of people in central Europe and the Orient for hundreds of years. This fish was domesticated and reared for centuries in ponds in China, where it remains an important source of food today. It was introduced into England in the early 1500s and is still a popular food there. Brought to North America in the late 1800s at the insistence of European immigrants, the carp was a traditional Christmas delicacy and the favorite aquatic food of these people.

Advocates of carp as a food fish sometimes sing their praises in rather flowery terms. One writer stated

> Long live the Queen. Don't ask if the carp is good enough for you to eat. Ask instead if you're good enough to eat carp. The fish has a heritage richer than your own. In its native Europe and Asia, the carp was the menu of royalty, a delicacy only the rich could afford. When it was brought to this country in the late 1800s, the carp was hailed as the superstar of the fish world, far superior to anything then swimming in waters of America. People all over the country literally stood in line to get carp and stocked them in every available pool of water in the United States. At last, everyone would eat like a king.

Another author wrote

> The carp's image as a polluter and a trash fish is hard to dispel, but it may be even harder to move stoic sportsmen away from another prevalent notion about this scaly denizen of muddy waters. Many anglers don't like carp simply because they are convinced that the damned things are hard, if not impossible, to eat. Nothing could be further from the truth.

Carp are economical and good to eat, according to another recent author from Iowa.

> The inflationary spiral has gripped tightly the pocketbooks of every American. As the cost of protein continues to escalate, there is a simple way to cut some food costs: utilize our over-abundant and inexpensive fishes as protein substitutes for more expensive ones. Expanded use of inland commercial fishes offers this potential as they are readily available throughout Iowa. Carp are relatively easy to acquire and are inexpensive. Carp are delicious when they are obtained from unpolluted water providing they are properly prepared. The carp's bad reputation is totally incorrect.

Carp has been the food of royalty. Respectful handling and preparation can make it a feast for anyone. (Courtesy, Wisconsin Department of Natural Resources.)

Carp should be used as a valuable resource according to one fishery manager.

> Say carp to many fishermen and they'll turn up their noses and walk away. But these hardy fish are gallant fighters and make mighty good eating besides. They battle as well or better than many of the more sought-after game fishes. When properly prepared, they taste a good deal better than some so-called game species. Still, because of his hardiness, his general disdain for artificial lures, and his ability to outcompete game fishes, the carp ranks low on the angler's preferred list. Even so, some folks will take the carp over his more esteemed cousins.

Readers who have never before thought of eating carp should consider that 16.1 million pounds of carp have been harvested during each of the past 10 years in 12 midwestern states and that almost every carp caught was used for human consumption. Part of this annual total (2.3 million pounds) is hauled live to three restaurants in Omaha and Lincoln, Nebraska, where local residents prefer the carp served there above any other fish. Can this many people be wrong?

Handling Carp for Good Eating

Walk along the banks of a stream or talk to boat fishermen, and you'll see the reasons why some freshly caught fish are not destined to become gastronomic delights. The fish have been thrown up on the bank to roll in the dirt, or they have died and been kept in a pail of warm water, or been held dead on a stringer in warm summer waters for some time. The most delicious fish of all are those that are freshly caught, properly handled, and cooked with imagination and a top-notch recipe.

Nutritionally, carp flesh is excellent food for humans. It is high in protein (16%), relatively low in fat (6%), and contains no carbohydrates. A 6-ounce serving adds only 213 calories to the meal. The fat in carp flesh, although not abundant, is the cause of the poor flavor that the fish has at times. Fats can absorb disagreeable odors from decomposing bottom materials or acquire the musty flavor of certain algae. Also, the breakdown of normal body fat when the flesh is improperly handled and frozen contributes to the poor flavor of the flesh.

When fish are taken from waters suspected of producing bad tastes or odors, sniff the gills. If the gills have a musty odor, the flesh will also taste bad. Strangely, not all carp taken from the same lake or stream acquire bad odors or tastes. Fortunately, carp may be purged of off-tastes and odors in 5 to 7 days by holding them alive in clean water or in the same water from which they were caught, provided that they are kept in nets or traps off the bottom muds.

If you want the best-tasting fish, bleed and gut it as soon as you catch it and place it in a cooler or on ice. Fish can be bled by cutting either the artery near the tail, or a large artery in the isthmus between the gills. If it is against the law in your locality to litter waters with fish entrails, place the whole fish on ice. Alternatively, remove the gills and internal organs, place them in a pail or plastic bag, and dispose of them after you return home.

If you do not have an ice chest or cooler, keep your fish alive as long as possible in a large-mesh bag or on clip-type stringer. If the fish is deeply hooked, do not remove the hook. The fish will stay alive much longer if you simply cut the line, leaving some leader material hanging out of the mouth as a reminder to remove the hook when you clean the fish.

Sometimes you may wish to freeze your catch for future use. To minimize oxidation of frozen carp, it is preferable to freeze the fish whole and ungutted. After it has completely frozen, the fish can be dipped in a mixture of water and salt (or water and citric acid) to form a coating of ice. This will prevent freezer burn commonly encountered under long storage. Another technique is to cut the flesh in pieces, freeze the pieces in containers, and then cover them with a liquid mixture consisting of a tablespoon of lemon juice per quart of water. These procedures ensure a good quality of flesh when the fish is thawed for future cooking.

Preparing a Carp for Cooking

Carp can be baked, pickled, smoked, canned, steamed, fried, prepared as gefilte fish, or put into chowders or soups. It can be ground and stuffed into sausages or made into appetizing fish spreads, patties, or pies. Each cooking method may require slightly different methods of processing. However, most preparations start with gutting and fleecing the fish, with either the head intact or cut off.

Fleecing

Fleecing is a method of scale removal. It is accomplished with a sharp filleting knife that is inserted just ahead of the caudal (tail) fin with the knife pointing dorsally (toward the fish's back) and the sharp edge facing anteriorly (toward the head). After the scales are loosened at the tail, the knife is used to separate the scales from the skin along the side of the belly. Then, with short, sawing cuts, the scales are removed along the side. The entire mass of scales can be lifted, leaving the skin looking clean and pearly white.

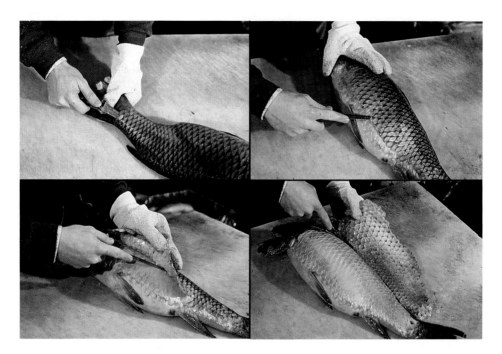

The large scales of carp can be fleeced off the skin as a single layer. (Courtesy, Wisconsin Department of Natural Resources.)

Filleting and Skinning

The fish can be filleted and skinned for pan frying, for use in chowders and soups, or for pickling. The filleting operation can be done with the head on or removed. The fish need not be fleeced or gutted before fillets are cut, although a fleeced fillet can be scored nicely, breaded, and then pan or deep fried.

To cut a fillet, place the fish on its side. With a sharp knife, start a cut directly behind the gills and extend it along the back. The cut is deep, to the vertebral column. Continue the cut along the back until it is opposite the vent. Then push the knife through to the belly side and pull it through to the tail. Lift the cut edge of the fillet with your free hand and, with forceful slicing movements, continue the knife cut around the ribs.

After you remove the fillet, place it skin down on a cutting board. Grasp the tail with the thumb and forefingers. First make a downward cut of the knife through the flesh to the tail skin, and then pull one way with the skin and cut in the opposite direction parallel to the skin. This will skin the fillet quickly and cleanly.

The reddish-brown flesh on the skin side of the fillet is often called the red muscle or mud vein. This special muscle is responsible for much of the strong fishy flavor and may be removed and discarded.

Boning and Scoring

The carp has a series of free-floating bones on each side of the body in orderly rows within the flesh. These bones are not connected to the rest of the skeleton, but are arranged in an overlapping series between muscle segments. Above the lateral line, there are 26 of these bones on each side, of which 20 are Y-shaped with various branch lengths and six are straight. Below the lateral line are 17 additional free-floating bones, four of which are forked. All of the free-floating bones are found in the flesh approximately one-third of the depth below the surface.

The carp fillet is scored by cutting into the outside of the muscle mass only deep enough to break the bones into small pieces. With a little practice it becomes easy to determine when the bones have been cut. To maintain the integrity of the fillet, and to keep the fillet in a single piece for cooking, the scoring cuts should never penetrate all the way through the fillet or to its upper (dorsal) and lower (ventral) edges.

If carp fillets are purchased in a fish market, they already have been either scored or processed through a meat tenderizing machine. Both methods break the free-floating bones into small pieces. Cooking oils subsequently soften the bones to the point that they are hardly noticeable while being eaten.

Other Preparations

Carp can be cut like a loaf of bread into steaks that can be smoked, barbecued, or pan fried. A fleeced and beheaded fish also can be cut down the vertebral column into right and left slabs with a band saw. In this case, the scoring cuts to divide the free-floating bones can be deep because the slab is held together by the rib cage and vertebrae.

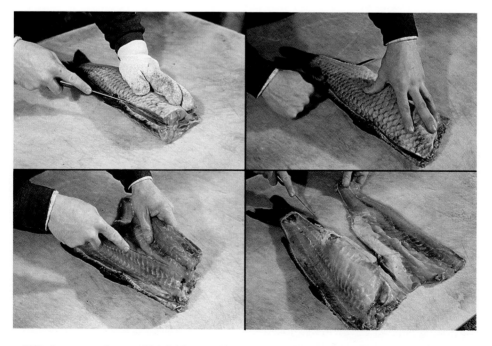

Filleting a carp is a rapid job if the knife is sharp. (Courtesy, Wisconsin Department of Natural Resources.)

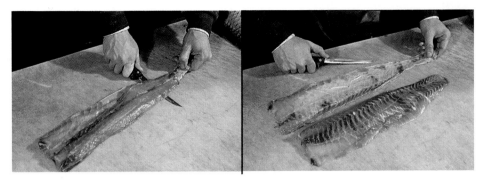

Once a carp has been skinned, less tasty patches of red-brown meat can be scraped from the lighter-colored flesh. (Courtesy, Wisconsin Department of Natural Resources.)

Whole, gutted carp can be baked, roasted with a stuffing, or smoked. The fish is bled and gutted, and its interior is scrubbed immaculately clean, care being taken to remove the dark-colored kidney material next to the vertebral column. The fish may be scaled or fleeced, and the head may be kept on or removed.

Cooking Methods: Baking or Roasting

Carp can be cooked in many ways, and an almost unlimited variety of recipes is available. It has been my experience that, with clean and careful preparation, carp can be made into delicious and appetizing dishes. An imaginative cook can adapt any of the following recipes to suit individual tastes. Perhaps one of these will entice you to try carp for the first time. If you already know that the carp is good to eat, try another recipe for some variety.

One of the favorite methods of cooking carp is to oven bake a whole fish, either fleeced or scaled, with the entrails removed. The head and tail can be removed, if desired. The fins are excised by cutting into the flesh alongside them and then pulling them with pliers; be careful to remove the basal bones along the dorsal and ventral midlines. Wash, and, with a stiff-bladed knife, scrape the fish inside and out and dry it with paper towelling. Then use one of the following recipes.

Baked Carp with Stuffing

2 cups soft bread crumbs	3 tbsp. melted butter
1 tsp. grated onion	2 tbsp. water
½ cup chopped celery	2 tbsp. minced parsley
1 tbsp. lemon juice	1 cup cooked rice
½ tsp. salt	½ lb. mushrooms

Clean and dry fish. Rub inside and out with salt. Mix stuffing ingredients and stuff fish, being sure to cover the exposed stuffing with foil so it does not brown too much. Brush outside of the fish with butter or margarine. Bake at 375°F, approximately 15 minutes per pound.

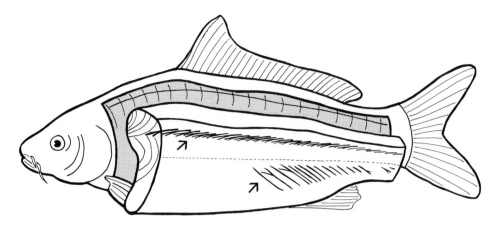

An important step in the preparation of carp is to break the small floating bones (indicated by arrows) that lie in the muscle above and below the lateral line. (Courtesy, Wisconsin Department of Natural Resources.)

Barbecued Carp

A surprisingly good method of preparing fat fish like carp is to broil them over hot coals. The fuels, each of which provides a distinctive taste to the cooked fish, may be charcoal or pieces of alder, oak, grapevine, mesquite, or hickory.

Fillets or steaks are placed on an oiled or greased grate 4 to 6 inches from the hot coals. Keep a water bottle handy in case the oil dripping from the fish flares up. After the fillet or steak appears to be nearly done on one side, turn it with a spatula. When completely cooked, brush with butter and squeeze fresh lemon juice over the fish. Use seasoning salt or regular salt and pepper to taste. Note: do not cook fish in foil. It is important to get rid of the excess oil from the fish for the best taste.

Broiling

There are several excellent recipes for broiling carp. You may wish to try one of these. Be sure to fillet and fleece the fish and remove the red muscle from the fillets.

Chinese Broiled Carp Steaks

2 lbs. prepared fillets	1 tbsp. lemon juice
¼ cup soy sauce	¼ tsp. grated ginger
¼ cup orange juice	½ tsp. oregano
2 tbsp. catsup	½ tsp. ground pepper
2 tbsp. peanut oil	1 clove garlic, minced

Place fish in a single layer in a pan and combine all remaining ingredients and pour over the steaks. Marinate for 2 hours. Drain and save the marinade for basting. Broil fish 4 inches from heat until done, basting with reserved marinade to brown both sides of the steaks.

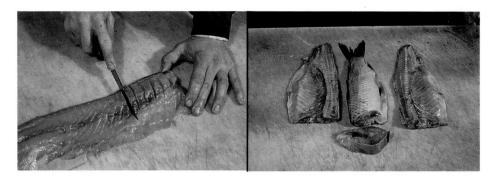

A good way to break the floating bones in carp is to score the flesh from the skin side (left). Carp can be prepared in the round, as cross-sectional steaks, or as longitudinal slabs (right). (Courtesy, Wisconsin Department of Natural Resources.)

Izaak Walton's Recipe

Here is a recipe for carp reputed to have been made up by Izaak Walton himself on or about 1653.

> When you have skinned him and cut off tail and fins and washed him very clean, take out his backbone and give him three or four cuts or scotches on the back with your knife. Broil him on charcoal, or woodcoal that is free from smoke, and all the time he is a-broiling, baste him with the best sweet butter with a good store of salt mixed with it. To this add a little thyme cut exceedingly small, or bruised into the butter.

Canning

To many persons who have tried it, canned carp tastes like canned salmon; the flesh is fairly firm and light colored, and the pesky Y-bones are softened with proper canning procedures. However, if you are canning for the first time, make certain that the bacterium causing botulism is killed. This requires adequate canning time at high pressure and high temperature.

The ordinary boiling temperature of water (212°F at sea level, and below 200°F at high elevations in mountains) does not kill botulism spores. When air is excluded from canned carp, the spores germinate and reproduce, forming toxins that are poisonous to humans. To prevent this, the cans of carp must be processed at least for 90 minutes at a pressure of 12 pounds per square inch, which will allow temperatures to reach 245°F.

Canned carp can be used for salads, patties, sandwich spreads, and baked dishes. Here are some processing tips that will ensure a good quality of meat.

(1) Carp should be fresh and of good quality.

(2) Never can carp in cans or jars larger than pint size.

(3) Follow instructions for the pressure cooker you are using. It is very important to properly pack the jars in the cooker, exhaust the air from them, and seal and cool them. If processed jars do not seal properly, they may be frozen and stored that way.

(4) Store canned carp in a cool, dark place. Light may cause changes in appearance and flavor. It is best to use canned carp within 1 year of processing.

Canned Carp

3 tbsp. catsup	½ tsp. water
4 tbsp. vinegar	2 tsp. salt
2 tbsp. cooking oil	

Clean and skin the fish. Remove rib cage bones. Cut into chunks to fit in pint canning jars. Pour the mixture of catsup, vinegar, oil, water, and salt over the fish. Seal with standard canning lids and pressure cook for *90 minutes at 12 pounds pressure.*

Casseroles

The flesh of the carp, either canned, fresh, or boiled, makes good casseroles or baked dishes. The fish flavors meld gracefully with other ingredients. Here is a good recipe.

Rice and Carp Loaf

3 cups cooked carp	1 tbsp. lemon juice
2 cups cooked rice	½ cup milk
2 tbsp. grated onion	2 well-beaten eggs
2 tbsp. melted margarine	1 tsp. salt
1 tbsp. minced parsley	Pepper to taste

Preheat oven to 350°F. Combine ingredients. Place in greased loaf pan. Bake for 40 minutes. Serve with fresh salad, small boiled and buttered potatoes sprinkled with parsley, and creamed peas.

Chowder and Chili

Carp were just made for piping hot bowls of fish broth mixed with vegetables. Try one of the following recipes.

Carp Chowder

5 lb. white baking potatoes	51-oz. can tomato sauce
1 3-inch onion	28-oz. can whole tomatoes
1¾ tbsp. salt	¾ tbsp. black pepper
4 lb. raw, boned carp	½ lb. butter
¼ lb. soda crackers	1 pint coffee cream

This recipe makes 3 gallons of chowder, so use a large kettle. Peel, quarter, and slice potatoes thin. Rinse potato slices in cold water until water is clear of excess starch, then drain them completely. Put the onion in a blender with water and reduce to liquid. Add onion and salt to potatoes, cover with water to the top of the potatoes, then add 2 more quarts of water. Boil until potatoes are soft. *Do not pour off the liquid.* With a potato masher, reduce about ¾ of the potatoes to a puree. Remove all fat from back and belly pieces of the fish. Cut the fish in chunks and add to the potato puree. Put whole tomatoes in the blender for 2 seconds to break them up, and add them to the potato puree along with the tomato soup. Cook until the fish flakes. Turn down heat. Put soda crackers in the blender, reduce them to cracker meal, and add hot water to liquify. Then add this mixture, along with pepper, butter, and half-and-half coffee cream, to the chowder. Add enough hot water to give the consistency of a medium thick soup. Simmer for ½ hour. Then eat and enjoy. Freezes nicely for future use.

Carp Chili

Fresh carp flesh that is processed through a food grinder to break down the bones and then panfried becomes crumbly, with much the same consistency as ground beef or ground pork. Carp treated this way is used in the following recipe.

1 lb. ground carp	2 tbsp. cooking oil
1-lb. can kidney beans	1 pkg. chili spices
1-lb. can tomatoes	½ tsp. hot chili powder
½ tsp. cumin powder	

Heat fish in oil until fully cooked. Add fish to beans, tomatoes, and chili spices. Add some hot chili powder and cumin powder to taste. Heat and serve with cheese topping.

Here are some notes on flavoring chili. (1) Leave out the hot chili powder or use regular chili powder if you like mild chili. Add cayenne pepper for a hotter chili. (2) Add more chili powder if you are not using the package of chili spices. (3) Onions, onion powder, garlic powder, and green peppers may be added to taste.

Dips and Spreads

Smoked or canned carp just seems to have been made for chip dips and cracker spreads. The delicious taste of the smoked fish mixes perfectly with the other ingredients.

Canned Carp Dip

1 pint sour cream	3–5 drops liquid smoke
1 pint canned carp	Onion salt to taste
1 cup salad dressing	1 tsp. fresh or dried chives

Mix together and serve with corn chips or potato chips. Surprise your guests. After they have praised the dip—tell them it's canned carp.

Smoked Carp Spread

1½ lb. smoked carp	Lemon juice
1 cup mayonnaise	2 tbsp. sweet pickle relish
Worcestershire sauce	

Remove skin and bones of the smoked fish. Run smoked carp through a food grinder, or chop it finely. Combine ingredients. Use as a spread on crackers or rye bread. One hundred pounds of this spread were prepared for an American Fisheries Society picnic in Milwaukee, Wisconsin, in August 1983. It all disappeared.

Frying: Cooking Tips, Breading, and Batters

Here are several tips for panfrying or deep-frying carp.

(1) Never overcook the fish. It should be moist, flaky, and steaming.

(2) When breading fish, do not mix salt and pepper with flour. Instead, make a Chef's salt of 1 cup salt, 1 tbsp. Hungarian or Spanish paprika, ¼ tsp. white pepper, ¼ tsp. garlic salt, and 1 tsp. freshly ground black pepper. Sprinkle both sides of the fish with this mixture before breading.

(3) Make your own fresh bread crumbs, preferably from French, Italian, or Vienna breads.

(4) If possible, fry in a mixture of half lard and half corn oil or butter. Lard has a high smoking point, which means it will crisp the breading at a much higher temperature than will butter or oil, without burning the fish. Because of the more rapid crisping at high temperature, the fish absorbs less lard than it would cooking oil.

(5) If you use cooking oil, panfry or deep-fry at 375°F. If a lower temperature is used, the fish breading will become gray and oily. A higher temperature results in dark-brown crispy breading but only partially cooked fish. At 375°F, the outside will be brown and crispy, and the inside flaky and steamy—just perfect.

Breading Carp

Dry boned carp fillets or scored 4-inch slabs of carp and place them in a paper bag containing all-purpose flour. Shake well to coat the fish. Then place the floured fish into a bowl containing 1 tbsp. cold water per egg that has been scrambled with a whisk. Place floured, egged fish into a pan containing Italian seasoned bread crumbs (or make crumbs from the dry seasoned bread cubes used for poultry stuffing by putting them in a blender). Pat crumbs onto the fish with the heel of your hand. Pan or deep-fry as recommended. Serve with lemon wedges and tartar sauce (see recipes for sauces).

Beer Batter for Fried Carp

1 cup beer	1 tsp. salt
1 cup flour	1 tsp. baking powder
2 eggs, slightly beaten	1 tsp. baking soda

Blend flour, salt, baking powder, and baking soda. Add beer and eggs and stir until batter is light and frothy. Dip boned fillets or scored slabs in batter and deep-fry at 375°F until golden brown.

Marinated Carp

Marinating carp in various solutions lends flavor, and may be used as a method of cold "cooking" of the fish flesh. The process of marinating fish is particularly valuable with species like carp that contain Y-bones, because the fish is chopped into small pieces, and the marinade helps to soften these bones. Two recipes are offered for your consideration.

Portuguese Marinated Carp

Prepare a brine of the following ingredients:

1 cup white vinegar	¼ tsp. thyme
1 cup red Burgundy wine	¼ tsp. marjoram
¼ cup vegetable oil	¼ tsp. black pepper
1 tbsp. salt	1 tsp. chopped fresh garlic
¼ tsp. cumin seed	½ tsp. lemon juice

Clean, fillet, and skin 2 lbs. of carp. On a solid block, with a light cleaver or heavy butcher knife, chop fish lengthwise as fine as possible. Turn crosswise and chop. In a large bowl or jar, submerge chopped fish in the brine for 2 hours. Remove fish, drain, and squeeze dry. The fish then can be prepared in two ways.

(1) Combine fish with enough flour to bind. Make into fish patties. Fry in hot oil until brown.

(2) Mix fish with eggs to make an omelet. Cook at low temperature until done. Has a very distinctive flavor.

Pickling

Small pieces of carp make excellent pickles (one of the oldest forms of food preservation known). In some regions, pickled carp has replaced pickled herring as an appetizer at dinner clubs and restaurants. Jars of pickled fish can be refrigerated where they will be good for weeks. They make unique gifts too, and can be dressed with sliced, stuffed olives and brightly colored strips of pimento and sweet pickles. Carp prepared this way make a tart–sweet, chewy delicacy.

Pickled Carp

For each quart of fresh carp chunks, dissolve ⅝ cup of pickling salt in enough vinegar to cover the fish. Let stand 4 to 6 days at about 40°F. Drain off salt solution and rinse thoroughly with cold water. Then collect

1 pint white vinegar	¾ cup sugar
1 pint white port wine	⅛ oz. pickling spice
Sliced onions	

Place alternate layers of fish and onions in sterilized jars. Place hot mixture of vinegar, wine, sugar, and pickling spice over fish. Refrigerate and let stand 1 week before using. This solution covers 4 quarts of fish. For variety, drain the juices after the process is complete and replace with commercial sour cream. A real treat.

Quiche

Excellent cheesy fish pies can be made with canned, previously boiled and boned, or smoked, boned carp. Try it for lunch, as a main dish, or cut in small pieces on a festive buffet.

Carp Quiche

2 cups cooked or canned carp	1 can cream of mushroom soup
1 cup shredded cheddar cheese	1 tsp. dill weed (not seed)
1 tbsp. flour	¾ cup sour cream
2 tbsp. butter	Pepper to taste
1 bunch green onions, sliced	2 eggs slightly beaten
1 jar pimento, chopped	1 unbaked pie shell

Sprinkle half of the cheese in a pie shell. Mix fish with flour and place in the shell. Sauté onions in butter until soft; add soup, sour cream, dill weed, and pepper, and heat until near boiling. Remove from heat, stir in eggs, and pour over fish. Sprinkle remaining cheese on top. Bake at 325°F for 30 minutes or until set. Let stand for 10 minutes before serving.

Roe of Carp

A female carp produces many small eggs; a large female contains up to 2 million of them. Carp roe has been used, as salted and processed green eggs, in salad dressing by the people of Mediterranean countries. Carp eggs can be used in other ways.

Preparation of Fresh Roe

To clean roe, remove all bits of viscera and connective tissue. Wash gently, but thoroughly, in cold water. Tie eggs in a cheesecloth bag and place in boiling water to cover. To each quart of water used, add 1 tbsp. salt and 1 tbsp. vinegar. Reduce heat and simmer roe for 15 to 20 minutes. Drain, cool, and again remove any bits of skin or connective tissue. Store parboiled roe in a covered container in the refrigerator. Use within 2 days.

Roe in Scrambled Eggs

Mince and sauté onions in margarine until the onions are translucent. Add beaten eggs, parboiled roe, salt, and pepper. Scramble the mixture. The amount of roe used may vary from just enough to flavor the eggs to equal amounts of roe and eggs.

Salads

As in other recipes, canned carp, freshly-cooked flaked carp, and smoked carp make good additions to salads. Try this recipe.

Summer Carp Salad

2 cups cooked, flaked fish	½ cup chopped cucumber
3 cups torn, raw spinach	¼ cup chopped green onion
1 cup thinly sliced celery	½ cup creamy salad dressing
1 cup drained bean sprouts	

Combine all ingredients, toss lightly, and chill. Makes six servings.

Carp sausage is but one of many tasty products that can be made from this fish.

Sauces

The secret of tasty fish is a good sauce. Deep-fried and panfried fish fairly cry out for tartar sauce. Here is a good recipe.

Tartar Sauce for Carp

1 cup mayonnaise
½ cup sweet relish
1 tsp. celery seed
Dash of paprika

1 tsp. yellow mustard
1 tsp. Tabasco sauce
Dash of Accent

Mix and chill for ½ hour.

Sausage

Ground carp flesh, when mixed with spices and cooked, provides an attractive and delicious sausage that is difficult to distinguish from other uncolored meats. Here is a recipe you may wish to try with breakfast eggs or hotcakes.

Carp Sausage

For every 1 lb. of ground carp, add ¼ to ⅓ lb. of beef hamburger, and 1 tbsp. commercial poultry and sausage seasoning.

Skin and fillet the fish. Partly freeze the fillets and grind them to a fine mash in a meat grinder. Add the other ingredients and mix well. Form into patties and store in the refrigerator for 24 hours. The patties can then be frozen or used immediately. Place patties in a frying pan over medium heat and fry 4 to 5 minutes on each side. Do not overcook. These cooked patties, when cold, make excellent sandwiches with lettuce and mayonnaise or tartar sauce.

Smoked Carp and Jerky

Most smoked meats, whether animal, fowl, or fish, are best when made from fat meats. For this reason, carp flesh makes one of the most delicious of all smoked meats. In the midwestern states, a substantial percentage of all carp caught is smoked commercially and smoked carp are available year-round in fish houses, grocery stores, and supermarkets. Many sportsmen, too, have discovered that smoking carp is easy, either in small manufactured, electric-powered smokers or in home barbecue kettles. Larger smokers can also be homemade from a variety of material ranging from old refrigerators to 55-gallon drums, concrete blocks, and plywood.

Procedure for Smoking Carp

Fresh, thawed, or frozen carp are fleeced to remove the scales. The fish are beheaded and gutted, and the body cavity scrubbed clean with a stiff bristle brush. The carp can be slabbed, steaked, or left whole.

Place the fish in a cold brine mixture for 12 to 24 hours: 12 to 15 hours for chunked or steaked fish, 18 to 20 hours for slabbed pieces, and at least 24 hours for whole fish. Then, rinse the fish in fresh water, pat it dry, and allow it to air-dry on racks until the raw uncovered portions of flesh form a "skin." You may, if you wish, rub the fish inside and out with a good vegetable oil at this time. Place the carp on the smoker racks skin side down, and put the larger chunks or whole fish on the lower racks.

Start the fire, following the methods prescribed by the manufacturer if a small commercial smoker is used. Burn small-diameter wood (hickory, apple, or maple) on top of 20 or so lighted charcoal briquets if a larger, home-made smoker is used. If the wood is dry, soak it in water for several hours. If the wood starts to flame, douse it with water; watch the smoking fish closely. Keep doors closed as much as possible to prevent over-drafting.

All smokers should have a good meat thermometer, either glass or electronic, mounted to supply an inside temperature of the smoker. Ideally, the temperature should be built up to 165°F slowly over a period of 4 to 5 hours, held there 1 hour to complete the cooking process, then reduced slowly over 2 to 3 hours. During the cooling period, place dampened wood chips (wet corncobs are good too) on top of the coals to give the fish that smoky taste and golden color. The smoked fish have an outstanding taste when they are fresh and hot out of the smoker and, of course, are excellent cold.

Once carp are smoked, the meat can be stored in a refrigerator in waxed paper for 3 to 4 weeks. It can also be frozen in plastic wrap or freezer paper and four or five layers of newspaper to retain that smoky flavor for several months. Be sure to thaw the fish slowly to get that fresh-smoked flavor to return. You can also remove the smoked meat from the bones and can it for longer storage time. Be sure to follow the canning instructions carefully after the meat has been smoked. Pressure-cook it in small jars at 12 pounds pressure for 90 minutes to prevent spoilage during storage.

Carp can be soaked in a variety of brine mixtures before it is smoked. For all of the brines, the salt should be of the coarse, noniodized, pickling or canning variety. Here is one of the better recipes.

Brine for Smoking Carp

10 lbs. carp	1 lb. pickling salt
2½ gal. water	

Keep the brine as cold as possible while the fish are soaking.

Carp Jerky

8 lbs. carp strips	1 cup commercial sugar cure
½ cup brown sugar	1 gal. water

Cut the boneless portions of carp into strips of various sizes. Soak the fish strips for 12 hours. Drain and soak in clear water for 1 hour. Then smoke slowly 10 to 12 hours until the fish is dark brown, chewy, and tasty. Carp makes jerky as good as or better than elk, venison, or beef.

Stir-Frying

Fish are preferred food in many countries. Fish consumption in other lands exceeds by several times that in North America. For example, Chinese cookery uses carp and other fish in many ways; among them are the following.

Stir-Fried Carp with Bamboo Shoots

1 lb. minced boned carp	2 tbsp. brown sugar
3 tbsp. oil	2 tbsp. dry sherry
1 tbsp. grated ginger root	5 tbsp. soy sauce
1 8-oz. can bamboo shoots	

Cook ginger in the oil for a minute or two. Add the fish and cook, stirring, until color changes. Add soy sauce, brown sugar, and stir. Add sherry and bamboo shoots (water chestnuts can be substituted for the bamboo shoots or added to them). Cook until most of the liquid has evaporated. Serve garnished with sliced scallions, or over rice.

Braised Carp with Hot Bean Paste

1 whole carp (2 lbs.)	½ tsp. monosodium glutamate
6 cups oil for frying	1 tbsp. soy sauce

1½ tbsp. green onion	½ tbsp. sugar
1½ tbsp. ginger root	1 tbsp. Worcestershire sauce
1½ tbsp. garlic	2 cups water
1½ tbsp. hot bean paste	1 tbsp. cornstarch
1 tbsp. rice wine	1 tbsp. water
½ tsp. salt	1 tbsp. green onion

Clean the fish and drain it. On one side of the fish, make a few diagonal cuts through meat to the central bone. Heat 6 cups of oil and deep-fry fish for about 1 minute; remove and drain the fish. Remove all but 3 tbsp. oil from pan. Reheat and stir-fry chopped onion, chopped ginger root, chopped garlic, and bean paste until fragrant. Add fish (cut side up), rice wine, salt, monosodium glutamate, soy sauce, sugar, water, and Worcestershire sauce. Cover and let simmer for 10 minutes. Add cornstarch and water and allow to thicken. Add 1 tbsp. chopped green onion. Mix lightly and remove to serving plate.

For family style cooking, fish need not be deep-fried. Decrease oil to 6 tbsp. and fry on both sides until golden brown.

Mexican Cooking

If you are hooked on spicy, hot Mexican food, try carp tacos.

Carp Tacos

1 lb. ground carp	12 tortillas
3 tbsp. vegetable oil	Shredded lettuce
1 pkg. taco seasoning	Shredded cheddar cheese
½ cup water	Taco sauce
Sliced tomato	Sour cream

Cook the fish in the oil until its color changes. Add the taco seasoning and water. Cook until nearly dry, stirring occasionally. Heat tortillas as directed on the package. To serve: Fill each tortilla with fish mixture, add shredded cheese, taco sauce, lettuce, and tomato, and top with sour cream.

Poaching

Poached carp are often prepared by gourmet cooks, and this recipe may be the one that intrigues you the most. A classic recipe is to poach the carp in Court Bouillon and to serve it with Bechamel Sauce (recipes follow).

Court Bouillon

3 lbs. carp steaks	2 bay leaves
2 qts. water	½ tsp. thyme
½ cup white vinegar	10 peppercorns
1 large sliced onion	1 tbsp. salt
1 sliced carrot	Handful celery tops
3 sprigs parsley	

Add all ingredients except carp steaks to water and bring to a boil. Simmer for 1 hour. Strain the bouillon and use it to poach the fish. Never put the fish steaks into boiling Court Bouillon. The liquid should be just warm. A 1-inch-thick fish steak cooks to perfection in 12 to 15 minutes from the time the bouillon starts to simmer. After the steak is cooked, set it aside in a warm place for 5 minutes so the fish becomes firm. Serve with Bechamel Sauce.

Chicken Stock Bechamel Sauce

¼ cup butter	10-oz. can chicken stock
2 tbsp. flour	Salt and white pepper
1 tbsp. cornstarch	Anchovy paste
1 cup light cream	Capers

Use a heavy-bottomed saucepan. Heat butter over medium heat until it starts to foam. Dissolve flour and cornstarch in the light cream, mixing well. Add to foaming butter, stirring constantly until thickened. Use low heat so it does not scorch. Stir in the chicken broth and cook for 5 minutes over low heat. Strain and keep warm until ready to serve.

Chef's secret! If the chicken stock is not strong enough, add half of a chicken bouillon cube and a very small amount of celery seed. For an exceptional Bechamel, add ½ to 1 cup of whipping cream, stiffly whipped with a pinch of salt. For fish, add 1 tbsp. anchovy paste and 1 tbsp. rinsed capers to the sauce before serving. (Always rinse capers under cold water to get rid of the chemical taste.)

Postscript

Now that you have read this far, it is obvious that a variety of different cooking procedures is available to produce many mouth-watering meals with carp. Carp may very well provide you with some of the best sport fishing you've ever had, but using your catch for food can only enhance your enjoyment. Certainly carp in North America are not going to disappear. Isn't it time all of us stopped criticizing them and put them to use?

Acknowledgments

I am indebted to several people and organizations not listed in the references for the tips, suggestions, and recipes compiled in this chapter, particularly Bob Becker, Everett and Mike Follett, John Gleason, Harry Thorne, Doretta Malone, Herb Pollard, the Wisconsin Sea Grant Program, the Texas Parks and Wildlife Department, and the Manitoba Department of Mines, Natural Resources and Environment.

I also appreciate the skills of the following employees of the Wisconsin Department of Natural Resources: Dean Tvedt, who captured the photographic sequences of dressing and fleecing fish; Georgine Price, who drew the illustration showing the location of Y-bones in carp; and Annette Praninskas, who uncomplainingly typed and retyped the several changes of this manuscript.

References

Ackerman, G. 1983. Canned carp cuts costs. Farm Pond Harvest, Winter issue.
Ambrose, D. M. 1983. Carp cuisine. Illinois Department of Conservation. Outdoor Highlights, August:11(15).

Deethardt, D. 1976. Crafty carp cookery. South Dakota State University, Agricultural Experiment Station. Pamphlet B 646, Brookings, South Dakota. 33 p.

Hacker, V. 1977. A fine kettle of fish. Rough fish, crayfish and turtles; how to catch and prepare them, and why. Wisconsin Department of Natural Resources, Publication 17–3600 (77), Madison, Wisconsin. 64 p.

Hekkers, J. 1981. Carp—twenty million Europeans can't all be wrong. Colorado Department of Natural Resources, Division of Wildlife, Denver, Colorado.

Mattingly, R. 1976. Great Lakes fish cookery—recipes for under-utilized fish species—alewife, burbot, carp and sucker. Michigan State University, Natural Resources Series, Cooperative Extension Service, Extension Bulletin E932, East Lansing, Michigan.

Miller, G. 1974. Time out for carp. Nebraska Game and Parks Commission, Lincoln, Nebraska. 7 p.

Regenstein, J. M., and C. E. Regenstein. 1983. Choose your title: kosher, minced fish, cooking and international fish recipes. New York Sea Grant Institute, Albany, New York. 31 p.

Reynolds, A. E., S. Tainter, and I. Bartelli. 1978. Great Lakes fish preparation. Michigan State University, Cooperative Extension Service, Michigan Sea Grant Publication MICHU-SG-78-100, East Lansing, Michigan. 16 p.

Sidwell, V. D. 1981. Chemical and nutritional composition of finfish, whales, crustaceans, mollusks and their products. NOAA (National Oceanic and Atmospheric Administration) Technical Memorandum NMFS (National Marine Fisheries Service) F/SEC-11, Southeast Fisheries Center, Miami, Florida. 432 p.

Promoting Carp

Tommy L. Sheddan

Would you like to discover a new fishing experience? An experience with one of the strongest fish, pound for pound, in fresh water? A fish that is abundant in lakes and streams and good to eat? If your answers are "Yes," you want to discover carp!

Here is a fish that should add to your total enjoyment of the outdoors, but it is presently the most misunderstood fish in North America. Promotion of this fish for sport and as a food fish is not difficult; sponsors need only stress the species' positive values. This chapter will provide ideas about how to encourage more people to take advantage of this abundant but overlooked aquatic resource.

Carp are gaining in popularity as a sport fish and food fish. To improve on this image, biologists and writers must learn the facts and talk about carp with a positive attitude. State game and fish agencies, most of which have their own magazines, should periodically publish carp articles that cover such material as rodeos, tournaments, clubs, fishing lakes, methods of baiting, suitable fishing sites, and cooking ideas. Many agencies are already doing so with good results. Agencies could also change the carp's image by putting this fish in the sport fish category. They could even add a creel limit, although there presently appears to be no management need for a creel limit to prevent overexploitation of this fish.

Everyone knows of expert fishermen who have become locally, nationally, or internationally famous through their magazine articles, newspaper columns, or television shows. These big-name fishermen could be a great help in dispelling public misconceptions about carp. Many of these promoters of good fishing would be eager to help, given the facts, and could convince the public that carp are worthy adversaries, strong in battle, and good to eat.

Television shows, featuring well-known personalities, could boost the acceptance of carp by running periodic segments on carp and carp fishing. The action can be fast and furious in a baited area, providing plenty of footage for the television camera. Such programs would do a lot to promote awareness of the sportfish potential for carp. Successful promotion of carp would provide some much-needed relief of fishing pressure now concentrated on other species. People who have no preconceived notions about carp, and young anglers especially, will accept new ideas about this fish.

It is up to fishery managers to let writers and the fishing public know that carp feed on insects and vegetation as do other favorite fishes. We certainly cherish the dining qualities of other bottom feeders such as catfishes, king crabs, and shrimp. Let us also put carp in this select group.

A clearing house for carp information would be helpful in promoting this fish. Groups such as the American Fishing Tackle Manufacturers Association, the

Carp tournaments are events for the whole family. (Courtesy, Tennessee Valley Authority.)

Sport Fishing Institute, and the Fish America Foundation would have much to gain by promoting a new sport fishery and the specialized equipment that goes with it. Europeans use rods and equipment for carp fishing that differ from the conventional equipment used in North America. A clearing house could gather a variety of information on fishing techniques, records, stories, tournaments, clubs, biology, cleaning, and cooking. This information could be packaged and periodically sent to outdoor and fishing magazines, sports writers, newspaper editors, and television producers. Writers and producers need stories and are constantly on the lookout for ideas.

While gathering material for this chapter, I corresponded with people from Maine to California and in several Canadian Provinces. One fact clearly emerged from this correspondence; there are a lot of people out there fishing for carp for fun and taking part in carp clubs, rodeos, derbies, and tournaments. It is a great fish for all ages.

Sponsors of Carp Fishing Affairs

Fishing tournaments or rodeos are popular means by which to promote carp and can be conducted by one or more groups working together to spread the workload and share initial expenses. Do not hesitate to approach large businesses. They have advertising money and are usually interested in becoming involved with community affairs and projects. Most of the following organizations or business groups have already sponsored one or more of these events.

Civic clubs
Chambers of Commerce
Hunting and fishing clubs
Radio and television stations
Newspapers
Regional magazines and papers
Sporting goods stores
Mail-order houses
Beverage stores
Local merchants and businesses
Fraternities and sororities
Food franchises or regional businesses
Professional men's and women's organizations
Fishing tackle manufacturers
Lake associations
Resort owners

Social Values of Organized Programs

Carp tournaments, also called derbies, rallies, contests, rodeos, and scrambles, are growing in popularity in the United States. They are often family oriented and, when combined with other activities, provide an all-day outing of fun. City and county recreation commissions hold rodeos as part of their summer programs. Senior citizens' organizations hold outings to get their members outdoors and socializing. Urban and children's fishing programs hold rodeos to teach fishing and provide summer recreation. Most rallies are annual affairs that grow larger each year. They are good ways to raise money for park improvement, charities, or whatever you wish. A fee usually is charged, and T-shirts or other prizes are given as awards for participation. National Fishing Week, usually scheduled in June, is a good time for a tournament with a theme such as "Take a Child Fishing."

There may be many disadvantaged persons or similar groups in your community who would like to fish but seldom get a chance. An outing for such groups is a public service that big business and local merchants are usually eager to support. Drinks and food usually will be contributed by local businesses. Prizes are not important in these events because socializing is the primary consideration for these participants. You only have to see the happy expressions and hear the laughter of these participants to know it is all worthwhile. If you have trouble contacting disadvantaged persons in your area, several of the following organizations can help identify those groups.

Big Brothers
Big Sisters
Young Men's Christian Association
Young Women's Christian Association
Boy's clubs

There is no age limit on successful carp fishing. (Courtesy, Joseph Evans.)

City and county recreation offices
Organizations for the physically handicapped
Organizations for the mentally handicapped
Foster and group homes for children
Senior citizen's groups

Planning a Children's Carp Rodeo

Family-fun rodeos can be held in lakes, rivers, ponds, swimming pools, creeks, or cattle tanks. There should be enough fish to give everyone a chance to catch at least one.

Baiting

In large bodies of water, baiting an area every third day prior to the contest will aggregate the fish. The more days you can bait, the better. Pellets of hog feed and shelled yellow corn are great to attract fish, but most food items will work. Don't be stingy with the bait. Scatter at least 100 pounds of corn or pellets for every 300 feet of shoreline. Scatter the bait a short casting distance from shore in water 5 to 10 feet deep and mark the baited area so fishermen will know where to cast. Check with state agencies for license requirements and special regulations concerning baiting and fishing contests. Excessive baiting in a small area could lower water quality, so use common sense.

Stocking

Small lakes can be stocked with additional fish. Contact your state or provincial fisheries biologist for assistance. Local businesses may contribute money to buy and stock fish. Small lakes can accommodate more people if different age groups are scheduled for different fishing hours. For example, anglers between the ages of 6 and 12 could fish in the morning; older anglers could fish in the afternoon.

Publicity

Publicity is extremely important. To get participants, you need to advertise heavily. Send a short but concise announcement to public service directors of radio stations, television stations, and newspapers, and be sure that all information is included and sent two weeks prior to the rodeo. Post notices about the tournament in schools, grocery stores, recreation centers, etc. Notices can be handwritten and then duplicated to save money. Put a picture of a fish at the top to draw attention. Print the fishing rodeo rules on the notice and give them out at the event; there should be definite rules for participation and conduct and everyone should have a copy. Notices should include at least the following information.

> Date and hours of the rodeo
> Alternative date in case of rain
> Place of tournament
> Participants (age-groups)
> Registration required before fishing
> Prizes
> Availability of rods and reels
> Availability of instructors for novices

Fishing Rules

Keep the rules as short and concise as possible but include everything the participants need to know. Here are some examples.

> Rodeo open to boys and girls ages 15 and under
> Rodeo hours are 10 am to 4 pm
> All participants must register, obtain a name tag, and wear the tag at all times
> Prizes will be given each hour on the hour for the heaviest fish (Such a rule may vary with the wishes of the local committee)
> No continuous casting (to prevent injury to participants and tangled lines)
> No artificial lures (to prevent injury and tangled lines); instructors are available if you need assistance
> Parents, please give children minimum assistance in catching fish
> The decision of the judge is final
> One rod or fishing pole per contestant
> Please do not litter
> Have fun!!

Prizes

Prizes are not necessary for a children's rodeo, but they will help to draw participation. You will have to remind parents to give minimum help. Fast-food restaurants will often give a free food certificate to each contestant. Trophies and merchandise are also good prizes. Bottling companies, bakeries, and meat packers will often provide free food for the publicity. Businesses who contribute food or prizes will probably give again the following year if you mention their names in the notices, on television, and in the newspaper.

Many waters can support good carp tournaments. This one was held at Lake Chatuge, Georgia. (Courtesy, Tennessee Valley Authority.)

Workers

There should be adequate volunteers to handle all phases of the tournament plus a few extras for last-minute needs and to provide relief. Sponsors may provide volunteer personnel, as may bass clubs, civic clubs, and churches. Include roving instructors who can help the inexperienced fisherman with proper knots, hook and sinker sizes, and bait and casting techniques. Make sure that these are experienced fishermen. Ask them to teach courtesy and sportsmanship also.

Equipment

Fishing tackle can be rented from Zebco, Post Office Box 270, Tulsa, Oklahoma 74101, phone (918) 836-5581, or you can buy low-priced equipment locally. A large canopy tent will provide protection from sun and rain, and serve as an identifiable operations center; one will usually be supplied free for a worthy cause. A checklist of other needed items follows.

> Tables and chairs
> Paper and pencils to register participants
> Two sets of scales (for small fish and for large fish)
> Pan or bucket for scales, to keep fish from flopping off
> Name tags and ink sticks
> Extra hooks, sinkers, floats, and line
> Bait (be sure that you have plenty)
> First aid kit
> Alarm clock if you give hourly prizes
> Pliers, screwdriver, knife, scissors

Bull horn
Camera to record the event
Paper towels
Toilet facilities
City or county permit if needed
Garbage cans
Dip nets for big fish

Policing the Area

To get the grounds clean after tournaments, offer prizes to those who pick up
the most litter. If fish will be taken home, you may want to demonstrate how fish
can be kept fresh and how they should be cleaned. Suggestions for cooking, and
recipes would be helpful.

Make sure that you know the state fishing laws concerning baiting, license
requirements, number of rods, etc. The city or county may provide a policeman
to direct traffic and parking.

Other Associated Activities

To create more interest in the tournament, consider additional activities for
nonfishermen. The following are possibilities.

Demonstrations of carp smoking and cooking
Carp cook-off with prizes
Fish fry (can be free or paid for by entry fees; the cooking may be
   sponsored by university or county extension services, civic clubs,
   etc.)
Making Japanese ink prints of fish caught
Local entertainment, such as musical groups, square dancers, or
   cloggers
Radio-controlled planes or boats
Children catching fish by hand in a wading pool (do not use fish with
   sharp spines or teeth)
Concessions, flea markets, arts and crafts

Carp Fishing Tournaments

Competitive sport fishing tournaments for carp may be similar to the family fun
derby. It can be bank or boat fishing or a combination. Here again, you can bait
areas (if it is legal in your state) or tell the fishermen how to. Entry fees returned
as part of the prizes awarded will probably draw more contestants. Rules should
be very explicit and strongly enforced to prevent arguments that sometimes arise
when large prizes are awarded.

The following excerpt from the winter 1984 issue of *Carp Newsletter Quarterly*,
written by Jim Rahtz, tells how one person developed a successful carp tournament.

Instruction time at a Missouri carp tournament. (Courtesy, Missouri Department of Conservation.)

I like to think of myself as a fairly good fisherman, but I'm no pro by any means. Primarily a carp angler, I never have felt the thrill of competition fishing and have been jealous of my bass fishing friends.

As the manager of lakes in southwestern Ohio, I decided to hold a carp tournament on 188-acre Winton Woods Lake. If enough people showed interest, I reasoned, maybe it would become an annual affair. The rules were simple. Each team of two anglers would pay a $3 entry fee. Two lines were allowed per person, three hooks per line. Fishing would be from 9 am to 1 pm. Winners were to be decided by total weight, with trophies and prizes of tackle given to the first three places and also to whoever (excluding the first three teams) caught the largest carp of the day. I sent out news releases and put up signs at the four park district boathouses. Normally the Bass Tournaments held in the park district have about 10 to 15 teams entered, and I was hoping for that many. The day of the carp contest, 21 teams showed up.

I was relieved of my first worry, the turnout. Now I could move on to my second worry: Would they catch any fish? At weigh-in time, those who fished the shallows proved to be the winners. The first-place team caught 13 fish weighing just under 20 pounds total, and nearly every team caught fish, for a total of 87 fish weighing 200 pounds. All the fish were released into a nearby pond to be caught again another day by the children and senior citizens for whom this pond is reserved. Everyone had such a good time that they wanted another tournament.

The second tournament (lengthened to 5 hours) drew over 60 anglers who caught 111 carp weighing a total of about 250 pounds. After it was over, we heard the same question: When's the next one? So we scheduled another for October. Cold weather had hit by then, and the 20 teams entered were only able to bring in 65 carp weighing about 100 pounds. Everyone once again had a good time, and we are planning a whole series of carp tournaments for next year.

If you would like more information on the tournaments or the park district, send me a line at the following address: Hamilton County Park District, 10245 Winton Road, Cincinnati, Ohio 45231, Attention Jim Rahtz.

The number of competitive carp fishing events seems to be increasing each year. Listed after the references are those known by me to have been held in 1983 or 1984. Most of these are annual affairs. Contact sponsors for further details.

Catch-Out Ponds

Catch-out ponds for carp are not widely publicized, but they exist in several states. Daily fishing fees average $2 or $3 per person, and many owners run jackpots on an hourly, daily, or weekly basis. Each angler can enter as many pots as desired; pots have typical values of $1 to $5 each. The prizes are awarded in several ways, such as for the largest fish, for the fish nearest a predetermined weight, or for the first fish caught after a prearranged signal. Prizes are also given by the owner for the most fish or the most weight caught during a given period of time. I talked to a fisherman at a recent rodeo who said that he won $17,000 in 1983 fishing in carp contests. Pay lakes exist in at least seven states: Indiana, Ohio, Missouri, South Carolina, Georgia, Kentucky, and North Carolina. Pond owners who wish to start a fee lake or restock their ponds can buy fish from commercial fishermen.

Promoting Carp as a Sport Fish

There are many organizations and clubs interested in promoting carp as a sport fish. Some of these were mentioned earlier in this chapter. In addition, there are individuals who have special interests in promoting carp. Some of these persons are listed here.

Ms. Jean E. Ward is an associate professor who teaches casting and angling. She is a recent holder of four International Game Fish Association world records, and 10 Freshwater Fishing Hall of Fame records for carp. Ms. Ward would be happy to share her extensive knowledge and notes on carp fishing. She can be contacted at: HPERS, Fairmont State College, Fairmont, West Virginia 26554.

Tom Krizan is an outdoor writer and sport fisherman with an avid interest in snorkeling and spear fishing. His address is: 2013 South Vine Street, Urbana, Illinois 61801, or phone (217) 344-6984.

A carp-fishing tournament underway in Missouri. (Courtesy, Missouri Department of Conservations.)

A communal carp fry makes a fine tournament finale. (Courtesy, Missouri Department of Conservation.)

Lefty Kreh is also an outdoor writer and sport fisherman who has lectured widely on angling. Write to: 210 Wickersham Way, Cockeysville, Maryland 21030, or phone (301) 667-4876.

Dan Gapen is a well-known author of outdoor books as well as a manufacturer of fishing tackle. For information on carp fishing, write to: Route 1, Big Lake, Minnesota 55309, or phone (612) 263-3558.

Ted Harmon is an enthusiastic promoter of carp tournaments and a championship carp cook. He would be happy to share his knowledge with you. Write to: Carp 1, 600 South Main Street, Rockport, Missouri 64482, or phone (816) 744-5570.

Promoting Carp as a Commercial Fish

Many commercial fish specialists feel that a constant guaranteed supply of carp is necessary before large-volume commercial consumers will be interested. This might best be accomplished by a regional cooperative of interested parties, primarily commercial fishermen and buyers. Fishermen must be made to feel that they are a very important part of the organization and that the cooperative will benefit them. They should benefit from a steadier demand and a price that will be more stable at first but that probably will increase once the buying public is convinced of the quality and availability of carp.

States that now contract with commercial fishermen for fish removal from lakes as a management program for sport fishing may wish to stop charging commercial fishermen for this service. This would encourage fishermen to catch more fish and to find markets for them, since it would give them a larger profit margin. The rising cost of most food should give carp an advantage in the marketplace. Carp also should be competitive in price with marine fish, especially in inland areas. Publicly funded schools, universities, juvenile homes, jails, prisons, retirement homes, mental health facilities, and food assistance programs are some of the potential markets for carp.

An easy part of the selling program is that carp are good to eat as well as inexpensive; they are high in protein, but low in fat and calories. Thousands of pounds of carp are used in carp sandwiches by an enterprising Nebraska food operation. Eastern and midwestern food markets sell smoked carp, some for as high as $5.20 per pound. Wisconsin alone sells between 3 and 4 million pounds of smoked carp each year, and there may be other states which sell even more. Canned carp is available from Ramer Fish Company, Winona, Minnesota 55987. Fish sausage made from carp is almost identical to pork sausage when prepared with pork fat and sausage seasoning and rolled in cracker crumbs. Pickled carp in sour cream is comparable to pickled herring. These are only some of the ways that carp can be prepared that are excellent eating. Several universities are working on recipes to promote freshwater commercial fish, but none that I know of are working specifically on carp. Elsewhere in this book, Vern Hacker has compiled a set of fine carp recipes.

A major problem of selling carp as a food fish is the species' questionable public image. Here are some ideas that might help change that image.

> Enlighten the public that carp are good food fish and the most
>   widely eaten fish in the world
> Publicize the fact that carp are bottom feeders like flounder and
>   shrimp, and that their main diet is insects (the food of trout)
> Stop applying the management term "rough fish" to carp
> Allow a name other than carp to be used in labelling of fish
>   products made from carp
> Encourage federal government agencies to assist states and
>   provinces in promoting carp as a food fish, and in developing
>   commercial markets for carp

References

Colorado Division of Wildlife, 6060 Broadway, Denver, Colorado 80216. Carp. (6 pages of carp history, biology, cleaning and cooking.) Free distribution.

Gapen, D., Big Lake, Minnesota 55309. Why fish carp. (46 pages of carp history, fishing techniques, and cooking.) Price, $6.95.

Kansas Fish and Game Commission, Rural Route 2, Box 54A, Pratt, Kansas 67124. Tips on carp and buffalo fishing and cooking. (2 pages on how to catch and cook these two fish.) Free distribution.

Nebraska Game and Parks Commission, 2200 North 33rd Street, Lincoln, Nebraska 68503. Time out for carp. (7 pages of information about carp, how to catch them and prepare them for eating.) Free distribution.

Ohio Department of Natural Resources, Division of Wildlife, Fountain Square, Columbus, Ohio 43224. Fish smoking. Publication 64. (1 page gives the basic information for building a 55-gallon drum smoker and preparing the fish.) Free distribution.

Tennessee Valley Authority, 115 Evans Building, Knoxville, Tennessee 37902. Sportsman's guide for smoking fish. (6 pages of instruction for building a smokehouse and preparing and smoking fish.) Free distribution.

Texas Parks and Wildlife Department, 4200 Smith School Road, Austin, Texas 78744. Consider the carp. (4 pages of information on catching and cooking carp.) Free distribution.

Wisconsin Department of Natural Resources, Box 7921, Madison, Wisconsin 53707. A fine kettle of fish. (64 pages of history, misconceptions, suggestions, and recipes for preparing commercial fish, turtles, and crawfish by cooking and smoking.) Price, $1.95.

Wisconsin Department of Natural Resources, Box 7921, Madison, Wisconsin 53707. Roughfish: underutilized, delicious (some), and inexpensive. (4 pages with facts about some good-eating and inexpensive commercial fish.) Free distribution.

Sites of Carp Tournaments

Colorado.—Lakeside Park Carp Contest, Post Office Box 24627, Denver, Colorado 80224. No other information available.

Georgia.—Lake Chatuge Carp Rodeo (held, in May 1984, at Towns County Park). Write to: Terry Taylor, Towns County Park, Post Office Box 444, Hiwassee, Georgia 30546. Five lakes in the Atlanta area are pay lakes and have derbies on a regular basis: Lake Ann at Lithonia, Twin Brothers at Tucker, Covington Lake at Covington, Williams Lake at Conyers, and Cedar Grove Lake at Fairburn.

Illinois.—The Midwestern Invitational Championship Carp Fishing Derby (held, in June 1984, at both Lake Springfield and Fox Lake in Ingleside). Write to: Bob Wolf, 37847 Douglas Lane, Lake Villa, Illinois 60046, or phone (312) 583-2657.

Kansas.—Sebelius Reservoir. Write to: Busch Western Carp Derby, Chamber of Commerce, North State Street, Norton, Kansas 67654.

Kentucky.—Write to: Land Between the Lakes Carporee, care of Jerry Conley, Tennessee Valley Authority, Golden Pond, Kentucky 42231. (The 1984 tournament was held in May.)

Maine.—Kivver and Carp Festival (held, in June 1984, at Taunton Conservation Commission Grounds at 3 Mile River). Write to: Urban Angler Program, Division of Fish and Wildlife, Field Headquarters, Westborough, Maine 01581.

Michigan.—Tournament held at the Public Fishing Pier on the Detroit River, West Jefferson and Rosa Parks Boulevard, Detroit. Write to: Catch a Carp Derby, Detroit Magazine, 321 West Lafayette, Detroit, Michigan 48231.

Minnesota.—Annual Coon Rapids Carp Tournament (held in June 1984). Write to: Tom McDowell, Hennepin County Park Preserve, 3800 County Road Number 24, Maple Plain, Minnesota 55359, or phone (612) 420-4300.

Missouri.—Write to: Carp 1, 600 South Main Street, Rockport, Missouri 64482. (The 1984 tournament was held in May.)

Nevada.—Write to: Fallon Carp Celebration, 76 North Main Street, Fallon, Nevada 89406. No other information available.

New York.—Write to: Bob Huckabone Carp Derby, c/o Bob Huckabone, 9 North Liberty Avenue, Endicott, New York 13760. (The 1984 derby was held in June at Grippen Park on the Susquehanna River.)

North Carolina.—Five pay lakes in the Asheville area have daily derbies from Memorial Day to Labor Day: D & D Lake at Fairview, Roberts Lake at Fairview, Spivey Lake at Fairview, Suttles Lake at Arden, and Wards Lake at Swannanoa.

Ohio.—Winton Woods Lake Carp Derby (held, in 1984, during May, June, July, and August). Write to: Jim Rahtz, Hamilton County Park District, 10245 Winton Road, Cincinnati, Ohio 45231.

Virginia.—Mudbass Classic Derby (held, in 1984, during April) at Virginia Polytechnic Institute. Write to: Department of Fisheries and Wildlife Sciences, Virginia Polytechnic Institute, Blacksburg, Virginia 24061.

Contributors

Dr. Edwin L. Cooper (Editor) is Professor Emeritus of Zoology at the Pennsylvania State University. He has been president of the American Fisheries Society and of the American Institute of Fishery Research Biologists. His many scientific and other publications include "Fishes of Pennsylvania and the Northeastern United States," which appeared in 1983.

Bruce D. Shupp ("Preface") has been Chief of Fisheries for the New York State Department of Environmental Conservation since 1980; before that, he served the state as fishery management biologist and leader of the warmwater fishery management unit. Prior to coming to New York, he worked for the U.S. Fish and Wildlife Service in the midwestern United States. He is past-president of the American Fisheries Society's New York Chapter and president-elect of its Fisheries Administrators Section.

Dr. Frank M. Panek ("Biology and Ecology of Carp") is a Regional Fisheries Manager for the New York State Department of Environmental Conservation. He is president-elect of the New York Chapter of the American Fisheries Society, and a member of the American Institute of Fishery Research Biologists and of Sigma Xi, the scientific research society. He is interested in the regulation of inland fisheries and in the world-wide biogeography of fishes.

Arnold W. Fritz ("Commercial Fishing for Carp") has been with the Illinois Department of Conservation for 30 years, the past 8 years as manager of the commercial fisheries program. He has been a member of the American Fisheries Society since 1956 and was president of its Illinois Chapter. He also is a member of the American Institute of Fishery Research Biologists and of other professional and resource management organizations. He has authored several scientific and semitechnical publications on sport and commercial fishes.

Ronald J. Spitler ("Sport Fishing for Carp"), an avid angler, has been the southeastern District Fisheries Biologist for the Michigan Department of Natural Resources during the past 18 years. He is a 22-year member of the American Fisheries Society and a past-president of its Michigan Chapter. He has written many technical reports and popular fishing articles.

Vernon A. Hacker ("Eating Carp") is a graduate of the University of Washington School of Fisheries. He retired in 1984 as Master Plan and Fish Control Specialist from the Wisconsin Department of Natural Resources. His career specialties were in studies of stream and lake trout and in large-scale chemical rehabilitation projects. He was executive director of the Inland Commercial Fisheries Association, which emphasizes the usages of rough fishes. He has written numerous articles, including a cookbook of rough fish recipes entitled ''A Fine Kettle of Fish.''

Tommy L. Sheddan (''Promoting Carp'') is an aquatic biologist with the Tennessee Valley Authority, Knoxville, Tennessee. He has been a member of the American Fisheries Society since 1968. His interests include the management of fish populations and their habitats.